HAWAII VOLCANOES NATIONAL PARK

A TRUE BOOK

by

Sharlene and Ted Nelson

ᛘ

Children's Press®
A Division of Grolier Publishing

New York London Hong Kong Sydney
Danbury, Connecticut

A giant tree fern

Reading Consultant
Linda Cornwell
Learning Resource Consultant
Indiana Department
of Education

Subject Consultant
Mardie Lane
Supervisory Park Ranger
Hawaii Volcanoes
National Park

Library of Congress Cataloging-in-Publication Data

Nelson, Sharlene P.
    Hawaii Volcanoes National Park / by Sharlene and Ted Nelson.
    p.   cm.   — (A true book)
    Summary: Describes the history, landscape, wildlife, and activities for
visitors at Hawaii Volcanoes National Park.
    ISBN: 0-516-20623-0 (lib. bdg.)   0-516-26378-1 (pbk.)
    1. Hawaii Volcanoes National Park—Juvenile literature. 2. Volcanoes—
Hawaii—Juvenile literature. [1. Hawaii Volcanoes National Park. 2.
National parks and reserves. 3. Volcanoes—Hawaii.] I. Nelson, Ted W.
II. Title. III. Series.
DU628.H33N45 1998
919.69`1—dc21   97-8232
                                                                          CIP
                                                                           AC

Printed in China
19 20 21 22 23 R 15 14 13   62

Contents

0 10 miles

0 10 kilometers

N
W — E
S

Kauai

Oahu

PACIFIC
OCEAN

Maui

Hawaii

Hawaii Volcanoes
National Park

Mauna Loa

Hawaiian
Volcano
Observatory

Kilauea Visitor Center

Thurston
Lava Tube

Kilauea Caldera

Jaggar
Museum

Halemaumau Crater

Hawaii Volcanoes
National Park

PACIFIC
OCEAN

An Island Park

There is a park on an island in the Pacific Ocean. In the park, you can look inside a steaming volcano. You can walk under giant tree ferns. You can watch the island grow bigger as molten rock flows into the ocean.

The park is Hawaii Volcanoes National Park. It covers 230,000

Molten rock from a nearby volcano spills into the Pacific Ocean.

acres (93,000 hectares) on the island of Hawaii. Hawaii is about 2,500 miles (4,000 kilometers) southwest of the United States mainland. This large island, and smaller islands to the northwest, form the state of Hawaii.

There are two volcanoes in the park. They are Mauna Loa (MAH-oo-nah LOH-ah) and Kilauea (KEY-luh-way-ah). They are among the most active volcanoes on earth.

Mauna Loa (background) rises high above Kilauea.

The First People

Hawaii's first people arrived there about 1,600 years ago. They came in big, double-hulled canoes from islands far to the south. The people steered north by following the stars and by watching the waves and the flight of seabirds.

Double-hulled canoes consisted of two canoes lashed together.

These people brought pigs, dogs, and chickens. They also brought coconuts and other seeds to plant at their new home. When they landed on the island of Hawaii, they found trees, ferns, flowering plants, and brightly colored birds.

Parts of the island appeared to be on fire. Sometimes the people saw lakes filled with glowing, molten rock. Sometimes the glowing rock flowed across the land. At other times, it splashed from the earth like a fountain.

The early Hawaiians believed in Pele (PAY-lay), the goddess of volcanoes. They believed that Pele made the rock melt and

The first Hawaiians planted coconut palms (left). They also saw lakes that appeared to be on fire (below).

Pele, the goddess of volcanoes

flow. Stories about Pele are still told in Hawaiian chants and in dances called hula.

One of the first scientists to study Hawaii's volcanoes was Thomas Augustus Jaggar. He went to the island in 1912. He thought that the area should become a national park. In 1916, Jaggar and a newspaper publisher, Lorrin Thurston, convinced the United States Congress and President Woodrow Wilson to create the park.

Thomas Jaggar holds a pipe to measure the temperature of molten rock. Lorrin Thurston is standing directly behind Jaggar.

Birth of the Volcanoes

Since Jaggar's time, many scientists have studied the park's volcanoes. Today, most scientists believe that Mauna Loa and Kilauea sit above a "hot spot" deep inside the earth. Molten rock, or magma, rises from the hot spot. When the magma erupts (breaks through

A volcanic eruption can be a spectacular sight.

the earth's crust) it is called lava. As the lava cools, it hardens into rock.

The park's volcanoes began growing over the hot spot

The constant flowing and cooling of lava caused the Hawaiian Islands to grow higher until they broke through the ocean's surface.

about 500,000 years ago. Lava first flowed onto the ocean floor and cooled. More lava flowed and cooled. The volcanoes grew wider and higher until their tops rose above the ocean waves.

Hawaii's Hot Spot

Hawaii's hot spot stays in one place while a part of the earth's crust moves. This crust is called the Pacific Plate. It moves to the northwest about 3 inches (9 centimeters) each year.

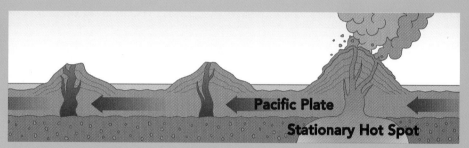

Pacific Plate

Stationary Hot Spot

The hot spot deep beneath the earth makes the park's volcanoes active.

Over millions of years, many islands have grown over the hot spot. Then they were carried away from it. Nine million years ago, Nihoa (nee-HO-ah) island (left) began as a volcano over the hot spot. It is now far away from the hot spot. It has been worn down by wind, rain, and waves.

The First Plants and Animals

When each Hawaiian island rose above the sea, it was bare and rocky. Then, from land thousands of miles away, very tiny fern seeds were caught by the wind. The wind carried the seeds to the islands. The seeds landed in

The first plants in Hawaii were ferns that grew on lava rocks after a volcanic eruption.

cracks in the rock. The rain watered them, and the seeds began to grow.

Over millions of years, the wind also carried spiders and birds to the islands. Some

Although the land once looked bare and rocky, trees and plants now grow throughout Hawaii.

birds brought seeds that were stuck to their feathers. Insects and snails arrived on drifting seaweed and wood.

On the islands, the animals and plants gradually began to

evolve, or change. Today, there are more than ten thousand native plants and animals found only in Hawaii. You can see many of them in the park. Examples

Ohia trees grow in the cracks of rocks.

An apapane drinks from the blossom of an ohia tree.

include a bird called the apapane (ah-PAH-pah-nay), the ohia (oh-HE-ah) tree, and the nene (NAY-nay), a Hawaiian goose.

The apapane is a small, crimson bird with a curved black bill. It uses its bill to sip nectar from the red blossoms of the ohia tree.

The nene is Hawaii's state bird. It has short wings and long legs. Instead of swimming in water, the nene likes to walk on lava rock.

The nene (left) is a type of goose that walks across lava rock (below).

Thousands of nene once lived on the islands. Then more people arrived with their cats and dogs and hunted the nene until there were few left. To save the nene, scientists keep some of them in a safe place to raise their young. Then the nene are let go to live in the wild. In the park, watch for road signs that read, "Nene Crossing." You may see the nene nearby, but you should never approach them or feed them.

Wild pigs destroy plants and can be dangerous to visitors.

Like cats and dogs, pigs are unwelcome in the park. Long ago pigs weren't kept in pens. Now there are thousands of wild pigs. They trample native plants and eat tree ferns. Rangers have built fences around the park's forests to keep the pigs out.

The Park's Volcanoes

Mauna Loa and Kilauea have gently sloping sides. The tops of these volcanoes are called calderas. They are shaped like huge, hollow bowls.

Calderas form when magma suddenly drains away from a volcano's summit, or top. As the summit caves in, rocks fall

A road leads around
Kilauea's caldera.

from its sides. Sometimes ash
and steam explode, leaving a
bowl with steep sides.

27

The volcanoes are often quiet. Mauna Loa last erupted in 1984. Sometimes they are active. Since 1983, lava has flowed almost continuously down Kilauea's east slope. Nearly 600 acres (240 hectares) have been added to the island.

Visitors are allowed to watch the eruptions from a safe distance. Stop at the visitor's center near the park's entrance to find out if lava is flowing and where to see it.

Kilauea's eruptions sometimes look like fireworks displays.

Mauna Loa, the park's highest volcano, is 13,677 feet (4,169 meters) high. Few people go to Mauna Loa. To see its caldera, you have to

hike 18 miles (29 km) over the park's trails.

Kilauea is 4,000 feet (1,219 m) high. You and your family can drive around the rim of its huge caldera.

Visiting Kilauea

Kilauea's caldera is about 400 feet (122 m) deep and almost 3 miles (5 km) across. Steam rises from the caldera's sides and rocky floor. In the caldera are large pits, called craters.

One of the craters is Halemaumau (HAH-lay-mou-mou). Its last eruption took

Halemaumau crater is inside Kilauea's caldera.

place in 1975. Some Hawaiians believe that Pele lives in Halemaumau.

You can take a short hike to the crater's rim. There are steaming, yellow sulphur vents inside the crater. On its rim,

Yellow sulphur vents can be seen inside the crater.

you might see fresh flowers placed there by people to honor Pele.

Halemaumau is surrounded by barren lava rock. Some of the rock is smooth. Early Hawaiians named this rock

Some lava flows make a smooth rock called pahoehoe (left). Other flows make jagged rocks called aa (below).

pahoehoe (pah-HOY-hoy). They could walk on it in their bare feet. Some of the rock is rough, like jagged lumps of coal. The Hawaiians named this rough rock aa (AH-ah).

A crater at the Thurston Lava Tube is filled with a rain forest. The crater's last eruption took place more than four hundred years ago.

In the forest, giant tree ferns tower over a trail. You may see the crimson apapane

The trail to the Thurston Lava Tube (above) leads through the rain forest. The happyface spider is too small for you to see, but this picture (inset) shows you how it got its name.

in the tree tops. A very small, native spider lives in the forest. It has a brightly colored "happy face" on its back. It is called the happyface spider.

You can also hike through the Thurston Lava Tube. The

Lava Tube is a dark, wet tunnel that formed during a lava flow. The lava's outer layer cooled and turned to rock. The lava's inner layer continued to flow. It finally drained out and left the lava tube.

Hiking through the Thurston Lava Tube is like walking through a tunnel.

Who Watches

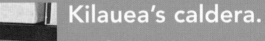

Scientists are always watching the volcanoes. They work at the Hawaiian Volcano Observatory. It is located on the rim of Kilauea's caldera.

Scientists measure the temperature of the lava. They also study instruments called seismographs. The seismographs are used to measure earthquakes.

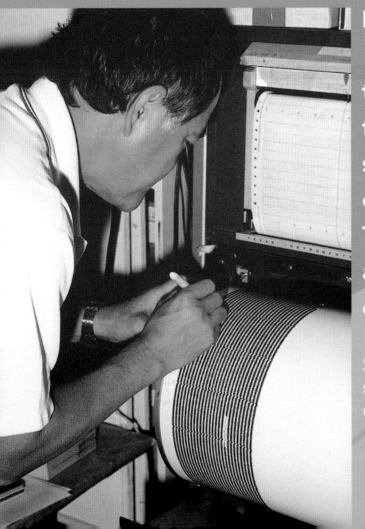

Seismographs show scientists when an earthquake has occurred.

the Volcanoes?

Earthquakes tell scientists that magma is moving beneath the earth's surface. When magma is moving, it means that there might be an eruption.

Scientists are also studying a new volcano named Loihi (loh-EE-hee). It is erupting beneath the ocean near the island of Hawaii. Thousands of years from now, it will become a new Hawaiian island.

Scientists measure the temperature of lava.

Kilauea's Recent Eruptions

In 1983, a crater on Kilauea's southeast slope erupted. Since then, lava has often flowed from the area. In November 1986, the hot lava destroyed homes and blocked a highway until it finally flowed into the sea.

The lava from Kilauea's recent eruptions has destroyed many homes.

Today, visitors can see this volcanic activity. There is a park road that leads to the ocean. You can see steam rise above the waves as hot lava splashes into the sea. At night, the lava glows red.

Visitors watch the steam rise as hot lava reaches the cool ocean.

Kilauea and Mauna Loa will continue to erupt until they are carried away from the hot spot. But that will be hundreds of thousands of years from now.

So, when you visit the park you too can see the fiery events that early Hawaiians believed was the work of Pele.

A visit to Hawaii Volcanoes National Park is a trip you'll never forget.

To Find Out More

Here are some additonal resources to help you learn more about Hawaii Volcanoes National Park:

 **Books**

Ching, Patrick. **Exotic Animals in Hawaii.** Bess Press, 1988.

Ching, Patrick. **Native Animals of Hawaii.** Bess Press, 1988.

Coste, Marion. **Nene.** University of Hawaii Press, 1993.

Fradin, Dennis B. **Hawaii.** Children's Press, 1994.

Lye, Keith. **Volcanoes.** Raintree Steck-Vaughn, 1992.

Murray, Peter. **Earthquakes.** Child's World, 1995.

Thompson, Kathleen. **Hawaii.** Raintree Steck-Vaughn, 1996.

Organizations and Online Sites

Earth's Active Volcanoes
*http://www.geo.mtu.edu/
volcanoes/world.html*

Giant world map with active volcanoes numbered for quick reference and corresponding links to each site, including photos.

Great Outdoor Recreation Pages (GORP): Hawaii Volcanoes National Park
*http://www.gorp.com/gorp/
resources/US_National_
Park/hi_hawaii.HTML*

Good information about volcanoes and the life that emerges around them.

Hawaii National Park
P. O. Box 52
Hawaii National Park, HI 96718

Hawaii Volcanoes National Park
*http://volcano.und.nodak.
edu/vwdocs/Parks/hawaii_
natl.html*

What to see and do, trail guides, upcoming events, news on volcanic eruptions, and more.

National Parks and Conservation Association
1776 Massachusetts
  Avenue, NW
Washington, DC 20036

Maui High Performance Computing Center (MHPCC) Photo Tour of Hawaii
*http://www.mhpcc.edu/
tour/Tour.html*

Lots of great satellite and land-based photos of lava flows, mountains, sunsets, wildlife, and other Hawaiian attractions.

Important Words

barren area where no plants grow

crimson deep, red color

crust the earth's outer layer

hull the frame or body of a boat or ship

mainland the largest land mass of a country

molten melted by heat

native plants or animals found in a particular place

sulphur element that seeps from vents in a yellow cloud

vent opening in the earth's surface

Index

Meet the Authors

Sharlene and Ted Nelson have visited Hawaii Volcanoes National Park several times, first with their children and, most recently, with their grandchildren. They have seen the fiery events and the changes that occur when the park's volcanoes erupt.

The Nelsons have written many articles and books about West Coast lighthouses, the Columbia River, and various children's topics. Other True Books they have written for Children's Press include *Mount Rainier National Park*, *Mount St. Helen's National Volcanic Monument*, and *Olympic National Park*.

LOVE'S QUIET CORNER

Laura Parrish

G.K. Hall & Co. • Chivers Press
Thorndike, Maine USA   Bath, England

This Large Print edition is published by G.K. Hall & Co., USA and by Chivers Press, England.

Published in 2000 in the U.S. by arrangement with Joyce Flaherty Literary Agent.

Published in 2000 in the U.K. by arrangement with the author.

U.S. Softcover   0-7838-8981-X   (Paperback Series Edition)
U.K. Hardcover   0-7540-4134-4   (Chivers Large Print)

The text of this Large Print edition is unabridged.
Other aspects of the book may vary from the original edition.

Set in 16 pt. Plantin by Rick Gundberg.

Printed in the United States on permanent paper.

Library of Congress Cataloging-in-Publication Data

Parrish, Laura.
   Love's quiet corner / Laura Parrish.
      p.   cm.
   ISBN 0-7838-8981-X (lg. print : sc : alk. paper)
   1. Large type books. I. Title.
PS3566.A7565 L73   2000
   813′.54—dc21   99-086878

To my family and friends
for all their support and encouragement

Chapter One

Perched on a stepladder, Kristen Edwards clenched her jaw as she grappled with the wooden sign. It was too heavy for her to manage alone, and she should have asked her aunt for help. But Grace was engrossed in finishing up an afghan, and Kristen hadn't wanted to bother her.

"Excuse me. I've been told you have a room for rent?"

The deep male voice came from behind her, startling Kristen so that she jumped, almost dropping the sign onto the porch floor.

"I'm sorry. Here, let me help you with that."

A large tanned hand grasped the bottom of the sign, and the man who had spoken came into view. Kristen gave him a quick glance, then involuntarily drew in her breath as her green eyes contacted a pair of blue, blue ones.

He had a face as tanned as his hands; strong, regular features; and dark chestnut hair that gleamed in the autumn sunlight. Her eyes swept down across the breadth of his shoulders and chest. He wore a well-fitting gray suit and white dress shirt — not the usual attire of a Fairhill resident.

Her momentary annoyance was wiped out by

another emotion — regret. She wished she'd brushed her shoulder-length, blond-streaked brown hair better and put on a more flattering outfit than faded jeans and an old T-shirt. But since it was Monday morning and the shop was closed, she'd decided to get the sign finished and hung.

"Thanks," she said, turning back around. "But I can manage."

"It's a heavy sign," he said calmly. His hand didn't let go its grip.

Kristen shrugged and made no more objections. He steadied the sign while she attached chains to the hooks.

When she'd finished, she climbed down the stepladder and stood beside him to observe the results.

" 'The Old and New Shop,' " the man read aloud. "Nice and direct. I'm glad you resisted using 's-h-o-p-p-e,' " he added approvingly.

"I *hate* those cutesy, quaint spellings," she told him. She'd done a good job on the sign if she did say so herself. The varnished pine board made a good background for the bright scarlet lettering.

"Did you just open your shop?"

Kristen turned toward him, moving back a little. Even though the fall day was turning crisp, she could feel his body warmth coming across to her. She shook her head, and an errant curl tumbled across her forehead.

"No," she said as she pushed the curl back, wondering how unkempt she actually looked.

8

"We've been open for three months, but I just got the sign finished today. It's mostly for decoration. Everyone in town knows we're here."

She smiled at him. He was one good-looking hunk of man: tall, but not overwhelming, with a muscled, athlete's build — and with a suspicion of a dimple at the left corner of his well-shaped mouth.

"What about visitors? If you hadn't put the sign up, I'd never have known about your shop." He returned her smile, and the slight indentation deepened.

"Our town grapevine is very efficient. I'm sure you would have soon. So you're interested in renting a room?"

He nodded. "The man at the Texaco station said it was still vacant."

Kristen's fascinated gaze left his dimpled smile and returned to his eyes. He must wear contact lenses. No one's eyes were naturally that blue. *Get hold of yourself, Kris,* she told herself silently. "Yes, it is. Would you like to see it?"

The man nodded and extended his hand. "Sure would. I'm Lucas Murray, and I'll be in town for a while. Do you rent for long periods?"

He enfolded Kristen's slender hand in his large, warm grasp. His hand felt good holding hers, she noted. Very nice. Lucas Murray. She tasted the sound of it in her mind and liked it. "I'm Kristen Edwards, and my aunt owns the house. But I don't think she'll have any objections to a long rental." Objections? Aunt Grace

9

would be overjoyed. It would mean a very welcome addition to their income from the fledgling shop.

Lucas Murray gave her hand a little squeeze, then released it. "Good. I'm in luck. I thought all towns had motels these days, but Fairhill, Pennsylvania, doesn't." His smile slowly faded to an expression of warm amiability.

"We don't get many visitors. It's quiet, but we like it that way," Kristen said quickly. His incredible eyes got nice little crinkles at the corners when he smiled, she noted, folding up the stepladder and leaning it against one of the porch posts.

She opened the heavy oak door with its stained-glass panels and led him into the wide hall. A stairway rose on the right, and beyond it on either side were rooms with invitingly open French doors. The room to the left had shelves and tables piled with colorful handicrafts, the afternoon sun striking gleams off glass jars here and there. The bookshop across the hall was comfortably filling up with both new and used volumes.

"Aunt Grace and I live upstairs, but we have two unused bedrooms down here." She walked briskly down the hall, very conscious of his presence behind her. Stopping before a room on the right, she swung open the door, then stood back so he could enter.

She watched as his gaze swept the spacious room, and then he nodded. "It'll do fine. May I move in now?"

He swung toward her, and Kristen blinked in surprise. "Well, yes, but don't you want to know what the rent is? And there's no private bath; you'll have to use the one down the hall."

That slow smile lit up his face again, the dimple flashing. "I'm willing to pay anything within reason. And a bath down the hall is fine. How about three months' rent in advance?"

Three months? Oh, that would be wonderful! She calculated swiftly. They could buy a full tank of fuel oil for the voracious furnace in the basement, with enough left over to finish paying for the last order of books. "That sounds fine." She gave him a wide smile.

His own smile hadn't left yet, but now he raised one dark eyebrow at her. "Don't you want any references, or at least some identification?" He reached around to the back pocket of his suit trousers while he talked, and brought out a wallet.

Kristen felt her face redden. Of course, she should have asked him for that at once. She was so caught up in this unexpected windfall, she'd forgotten. She pushed down the thought that tried to surface, telling her that his looks, his physical presence, had affected her too. She cleared her throat. "Of course."

She glanced at the driver's license picture he displayed for her, then at his face again. It didn't do him justice, but it was clear enough for identification. "You seem to match the picture all right."

"Do you always trust strangers like this?" His well-shaped mouth quirked upward, making her blush deepen. He moved across the room to glance out the wide window opening onto the side yard. "It could be dangerous, you know."

Kristen still stood in the doorway, considering his words. "No, of course, I don't," she told his broad back. Her instincts told her Lucas Murray posed no threat. Not the kind he meant, anyway. "If Joe Roberts sent you, you're okay," she added. "He's an infallible judge of character."

He gave her a quick glance, then walked to the big double bed covered with a white-sprigged spread and poked it experimentally. "I like a firm mattress," he said approvingly. He glanced up at the carved walnut headboard, then over at the matching bureau and chest of drawers. "This furniture belongs in an antique shop — or a museum. Aren't you afraid to trust it to the tender mercies of renters?"

There was that word *trust* again. No, she wasn't afraid to trust him with Aunt Grace's beautiful furniture, she realized. "All the furniture in the house is old. My aunt inherited it from my grandparents, who had it handed down from their parents. I guess we've just always taken it for granted."

Lucas Murray ran one hand appreciatively over a carved footpost. "You sound as if you've lived here all your life."

Kris's eyes met his again, and she nodded. "I

have — up until a few years ago. I've lived with Aunt Grace since my parents were killed in an accident when I was five. I went to college in Baltimore, then lived and worked there for the last three years." Her distaste came through, making her voice sharp.

"Baltimore's a nice city," he offered, coming to stand beside her again. "I'm from Pittsburgh — which has improved a lot in recent years, since they renovated so much of the city."

"I guess so — if you like cities. I don't."

"Don't you miss the big-city amenities?" His voice held a genuine curiosity.

Kristen shook her head. "No. If I get a yen for a museum or a fancy restaurant, I can always spend a day or a weekend in Baltimore; we're only sixty miles away. We've been so busy with the shop I haven't had time to miss anything."

"Is the population large enough to keep you in business?"

Kristen's eyes widened with surprise at this last remark. He sounded genuinely interested. He seemed to be a nice man, and he was going to be their renter for the next few months. And that was all, she reminded herself.

"Oh, yes, Fairhill is bigger than it looks. The town itself is small, but there are a lot of new houses on the outskirts. We have a large farm population too."

"That's interesting." His deep, vibrant voice was thoughtful. "So people still have money to spend on books and crafts, do they? Even with the depressed farm economy." He moved away from her, back into the hall.

Kristen closed the door and fell into step with him. She nodded. "This is also a consignment shop, and we're beginning to get quite a selection. But a lot of farm wives work these days, so they don't have time for needlework — or even all the family cooking and baking."

He turned again, giving her another interested look. "You sell food too?"

"I've always liked to cook, and I make jams and preserves. I take orders for specialty breads and other baked items. Oh, there's Aunt Grace now."

She felt a rush of relief at the sight of the older woman, realizing she was still much too aware of the man walking beside her. Kristen performed the introductions, and Grace Talbot shook hands firmly, her hazel eyes giving their new tenant a shrewd glance.

"What brings you to these parts, Mr. Murray?" She pushed back her short, brown hair, now liberally mixed with gray.

Kristen wondered suddenly why she hadn't thought to ask that question. *Because you were too busy noticing his wonderful smile and those blue eyes,* she answered herself.

Lucas gave Grace a smile. "Business. It's a pretty town. A little sleepy and slow, but otherwise nice."

"And that's exactly what we like about it," Kristen said, realizing her voice sounded a little defensive at his implied criticism.

He turned his smile on her, his dimple totally in evidence. "I guess it takes all kinds." His voice sounded amused.

"Weather's getting a little nippy — maybe have frost tonight," Grace said briskly. "Would you like a cup of coffee, Mr. Murray?"

"That sounds great. I'll go get my car and bring in my bags first."

"Sure enough. Kitchen's all the way at the end of the hall." Grace watched as he went out the front door. "Now, where do you suppose he sprang from?" she asked her niece thoughtfully.

"Pittsburgh, Aunt Grace," Kristen said, striving for a light, unconcerned tone. The older woman was no slouch at picking up on things, and without analyzing why, Kristen didn't want her to know how instantly she'd been attracted to their new roomer.

"That's not what I mean." Both women walked back toward the kitchen. "What's he doing here?"

"Business, he said." Kristen went through the open door into the big square room, and over to the range to put the kettle on. The top of the range was divided in half, with four electric burners on the right, and the left side for wood or coal.

"In *this* town?" Her aunt's tone was incredulous as she got down mugs. "Not unless he's planning to buy out someone — heard any rumors?"

Kristen reached into the basket beside the stove and picked out several pieces of wood while she thought. They'd kept the fire going all day the last two weeks. Doing so saved on oil, since Grace had an ample woodlot on her twenty acres. "No," Kristen finally said, lifting a stove lid and sliding the wood in. "Haven't heard a thing."

"Can't imagine something like that not getting around. Ronald Metcalf's been ailing. Reckon he plans to sell the hardware store?"

At the thought of the man whose footsteps she now heard heading toward his room owning and operating a hardware store, Kristen gave a hoot of laughter. "Aunt Grace, be serious!"

"You're right," the other woman agreed. "Not the type, is he?"

Chapter Two

Lucas carried two large leather bags to the room he'd just rented. His face wore a thoughtful expression as he placed them on the bright braided rug covering the floor.

He hadn't paid too much attention to Marian Dean's crisp, annoyed account of how her former partner had decided to give up her promising real estate career to bury herself in Fairhill. He'd been more interested in the area as a possible location for his newest project. Although small, it was only sixty miles from Baltimore, and like all towns that close to a large metropolitan area, it wouldn't be long before it started growing.

A scouting drive this morning had fired his enthusiasm, and he was eager to begin searching for sites. But the brief conversation with Kristen Edwards had whetted his interest in her.

When he'd come up the steps of the big old house to find her standing on the ladder and trying to hang that sign, he'd been surprised at the immediate attraction he felt.

Into his mind came the image of a piquant, fair-skinned face with sea-green eyes, framed by that mop of long, curly blond-brown hair.

Leaving his door open, he headed toward the kitchen. Halfway down the hall, he could smell the good scents of fresh coffee and something spicy, mixed with the fragrance of burning wood.

For a moment he was back in his boyhood, at his grandparents' farm, and an unexpected feeling of compunction struck him. He shrugged it off. He wasn't going to do any harm to these two women, or the town, either. No harm at all.

He walked through the open door and instantly approved of the red-checked curtains at the small-paned windows and the cheerful, old-fashioned charm of the room. Kristen was bent over a wood range, taking something out of the oven that gave off the spicy scent. Her aunt poured coffee into three white mugs set out on a red-checked tablecloth. A large yellow tiger cat slept on a rug beside the stove.

"Is there any chance I could get board here as well as a room?" he asked genially as he seated himself in the maple chair the older woman indicated. "Or would that be asking too much?" The cat opened one amber eye and gave Lucas a cursory glance, then went back to sleep.

Grace and Kristen exchanged looks. They'd never discussed this idea when they'd decided to rent the room, but why not? They were both hearty eaters and cooked for themselves. One more wouldn't make any difference. And the unspoken thought was there between them that every little bit of income would help right now.

18

Kristen had stretched things a bit when she'd said the store was doing well. It was barely making expenses, and she lived in fear that their fledgling enterprise was going to die aborning. It had been her idea, after all, and she had to make it work. She knew Marian was expecting the shop to fail and was sure she'd come back to Baltimore and the realty company she'd left a few months ago. She grimaced at the thought.

"I don't see why that couldn't be arranged, do you, Kris?" the older woman asked.

Kristen, cutting the crumb cake into squares, glanced up. "All right by me."

Grace turned to Lucas. "That is, if you're not too particular about the food. Plain country cooking is our style."

Lucas poured thick, real cream into his coffee. "That sounds fine to me." Life here in Fairhill was shaping up to be a lot more enjoyable than he'd imagined possible just a couple of hours ago.

A week later Grace and Kristen were preparing lunch in the kitchen when the shop bell dinged. Grace smiled wryly. "Wouldn't you know it? Not a soul all morning. We should have closed for lunch."

"What? And maybe lose our only customer today?" Kristen's voice was only half teasing, and her anxiety came through. "I'll go, Aunt Grace, since you've already started lunch." She ran her fingers through her mop of curly hair and pulled down the heathery green sweater she wore with her jeans.

It was nice to be able to dress casually, she thought, going through the hall door they'd left ajar. That was one more reason to be glad she wasn't still involved in the real estate business. She was very glad to get away from tailored suits and discreet strands of pearls.

Lucas Murray, his back to her, was hanging dripping rain gear on the coat tree near the front door. Today he wore navy slacks and a blue pullover sweater that matched his eyes.

Kristen paused, trying to ignore the way her heart thumped, then began to beat faster. "Oh, it's you."

He turned to face her. "Sorry to disappoint you," he said, his dimple showing as his mouth began to turn up in a smile.

Kristen hoped her expression looked as casually friendly as his own. "No insult intended. I just thought you were a customer."

"I might be," he said, glancing through the open French doors into the bookshop. "I'm out of reading material, and the drugstore doesn't have much of a selection."

Kristen's smile felt frozen in place. "Did you try the variety store?"

"No. I decided I'd already had enough rain for one morning without walking around the square. Do you always try to discourage business?" he asked curiously, moving a step closer to her.

She shook her head, resisting her impulse to

move back a corresponding step. It was the first time since the day he'd moved in a week ago that she'd been alone with Lucas. "I hope not," she said lightly, gesturing toward the bookshop. "I don't know your preferences, but feel free to browse."

"What, no signs announcing if you don't intend to buy, don't handle the merchandise?"

He didn't move any closer to Kristen. In spite of her vow just a moment ago, she was grateful for that.

"Absolutely not! I'm a confirmed browser, and I always assume everyone else is too. How else can you tell if you want a book?"

"Do you have any suspense novels or westerns?" Lucas turned to glance again through the open door leading to the bookstore.

"Lots of both. They're my biggest sellers. At least to the men," she amended.

"What about women?"

She smiled slightly. "Romances are the most popular with women, although they buy suspense novels too. But not many westerns."

"Well, I guess I'll see what I can find." He turned fully now to go into the bookshop.

Kristen cleared her throat self-consciously. "Lucas, you don't have to buy the books, since you're staying here. Just pick out a couple and exchange them for others when you're finished."

He paused again, one foot over the threshold. He raised an eyebrow. "See, there you go, hurting your business again." His voice was half joking, but with a serious undertone that made her think, suddenly, that he would be a formidable adversary. He seemed genuinely concerned about what he considered her lack of business acumen.

"Don't worry, I don't do this with all my customers. Aunt Grace and I were just about to have lunch — care to join us?" Lucas's board arrangement included only dinner and breakfast, but Grace was fixing a big pot of corn chowder; there'd be plenty.

He turned back around. "You've talked me into it. I'm sick of fast-food lunches. And some of that wonderful coffee would be great on a day like this." He followed Kristen down the hall.

"It wasn't a customer, it was Lucas," Kristen announced as they entered the kitchen. "He's going to have lunch with us."

Grace, stirring the chowder at the stove, glanced up, a welcoming smile on her face. "Sit down, Lucas. Nasty day out."

"I'll set the table," Kristen said quickly. "Coffee, everyone?"

"You bet!" Lucas said fervently.

Grace laughed, a surprisingly young sound. "Why not? I can use a lot of caffeine on a day like this. How's your business going, Lucas?"

Kristen's hand froze on the coffeepot, wondering how Lucas would react to her aunt's bluntness, even though she, too, was curious about what he was doing in Fairhill.

She heard the scrape of Lucas's chair being

pulled out. "I'm getting there," he answered calmly, nothing in his voice indicating he was upset by the question. He apparently didn't intend to expand on it, though, she concluded as she poured the coffee and laid out silverware.

"Not too many business opportunities in a little burg like Fairhill," Grace continued, ignoring his reticent reply. "Town could use some new blood."

Kristen brought the bowls of savory corn chowder to the table, her eyes briefly meeting Lucas's intensely blue gaze; then she sat down in her usual place opposite him.

Lucas helped himself to a slice of homebaked whole-wheat bread and stirred plenty of cream into his coffee. "Probably so," he observed finally. "Most small towns could, I think. They tend to get ingrown and complacent."

Grace nodded vigorously. "You're absolutely right. The young people with any ambition move away to a city when they finish school. Can't say that I blame them. There's not much going on here."

Kristen felt a small shock of surprise. She hadn't known her aunt held these views. She frowned and stirred her coffee vigorously. It spilled over onto the checked cloth, and she reached for a napkin from the holder in the middle of the table.

"That's exactly why I like it here," Kristen said. "Cities have entirely too much going on — too much crime, too much traffic, too many peo-

23

ple. I've had enough of all that to last me a life-time."

Kristen lifted her mug to her mouth, her green eyes challenging. Her aunt looked fondly amused, and Lucas gave her a quick glance. "Something in both viewpoints, I guess," he said, digging into his chowder.

Kristen took a deep breath, feeling a little embarrassed. She'd overreacted, she knew. She was touchy about this subject. She felt relieved that Lucas and Grace kept the talk casual during the rest of the meal.

Lucas finished his coffee and pushed his chair back. "Guess I'd better do some paperwork. All right if I pick up a couple of books on the way? I'll pay you for them tonight." He addressed his question to Kristen.

"Of course," she answered a little stiffly. She didn't repeat her earlier statement that he could read them without buying. If he wanted to pay, fine. They could certainly use the cash.

She watched him go, feeling a stab of disappointment and irritation with herself for her sharp words. She'd wanted to get better acquainted with Lucas. She'd wanted to move things forward between them so that he might be closer to asking her out, she admitted.

She shrugged. She'd never lacked for male companionship in Baltimore, and Brent Allan had wanted to take her out several times since she'd returned to Fairhill. She should have taken him up on his offers. Everyone needed to get out a little, she told herself as she helped her aunt clear away the lunch dishes.

She hadn't met any men remotely as attractive as Lucas since she'd been here. She doubted if there *were* any men in town who could compete with him, but the next time anyone halfway interesting asked her out, she would accept.

She darted her aunt a sideways glance. "I didn't know you considered Fairhill to be in such bad shape, Aunt Grace. I thought you enjoyed living here."

Grace stacked the dishes in the sink and turned on the hot-water tap. "I do, Kris, but that doesn't mean I think it's perfect. Like most places, it could stand some improvement."

"I think it's fine just like it is. After living in Baltimore all those years, I don't mind a thing about it."

Grace laughed again, squeezing her niece's shoulder. "Kristen, I swear, sometimes you sound like an old reactionary instead of a sharp-as-a-tack young woman! Maybe Fairhill isn't good for you."

Kristen felt a moment of alarm. "You're not tired of our partnership already?" She intended for her voice to sound teasing, but a slight wobble spoiled that effect. This town, this old house, and this enterprise they were engaged in meant everything to her.

Grace gave her a sharp glance. "Of course not. I'm having the time of my life. But I'm afraid you may be digging yourself into a rut."

25

Kristen shook her head vigorously. "No, I'm not. This is what I want to do, Aunt Grace. I've loved Fairhill all my life, and it hasn't changed over the years. That's why I can't stand the thought of having it spoiled by any so-called improvements."

Her aunt's expression was a mixture of emotions — part relief, and part puzzlement and concern. "Not all changes are bad, honey."

The shop bell dinged, and Kristen turned. "That *has* to be a real customer this time. I'll go," she said quickly. She hurried to the shop, not answering her aunt's last statement. She didn't want to argue, but she was far from convinced the older woman was right.

Grace's last remarks had surprised and unsettled her. She'd assumed her aunt was content with Fairhill or she wouldn't have stayed all these years. *Don't make such a big deal out of it,* she advised herself.

Lucas wasn't in the bookshop. He must have picked his books out in a hurry. Kristen summoned a bright smile for Celia Donald, who'd braved the weather with her two preschoolers and a shopping bag of paperbacks.

"I see you have a lot of books to trade today," she told the woman brightly. "You're in luck — we got a bunch of new trades in this week, by some of your favorite authors."

Kristen settled the two little girls in the children's corner, complete with small, brightly colored wooden chairs and a table of picture books to keep kids happy while their mothers browsed the shelves. That had been a good idea, she congratulated herself, as she sorted through the books Celia had brought in. She'd had more than one favorable comment on it.

The business was picking up; there was no reason to think it wouldn't continue. They were having a rough time financially right now, but they'd make it — they *would!* If they hadn't opened the shop, her aunt would have lost the house when she was forced into early retirement by the conglomerate that had taken over Fairhill Hospital and brought in their own people — after she'd put in twenty-five years as an excellent dietitian.

Kristen curled her lip. Just another example of big-city thinking! She opened a book flap and stamped *The Old and New Shop* inside. In high school she'd gotten bored with Fairhill and couldn't wait to get away to college. She'd liked her career the first year or two. But then the hectic pace of the real estate business started getting to her, and her small-town roots resurfaced.

When her aunt had told her she planned to put her big Victorian house on the market because she couldn't afford to keep it on her hospital retirement, starting a shop had seemed to Kristen like the answer to both their problems. She knew her aunt loved the house and so did she, but Grace was ten years too young to collect Social Security, and jobs were scarce for women her age in Fairhill.

The idea had hit Kristen with the force of an explosion. Her aunt did beautiful needlework; the house was full of her creations. Kristen liked to cook and bake. Both she and Grace loved books, and Kristen's business degree would come in handy with the paperwork and accounting. So the Old and New Shop had been conceived.

And she *wouldn't* get sick of living here and running the shop! She was happy as a clam in this pleasant, quiet little town, where nothing changed from one year to the next. And that was the way she wanted it to stay. Kristen began sorting books rapidly.

There was nothing to get upset about. Even if Lucas Murray planned to start a business here, which seemed unlikely, it wouldn't change things. She smiled as she remembered the hardware store idea she and Grace had discussed. No, that wouldn't suit him — but what would?

Chapter Three

Lucas went back to his room, carrying the two books he'd chosen from the bookshop. He was beginning to realize Kristen was a complex person. Her looks and manner were as up-to-date as tomorrow, but her attitudes about life were totally unrealistic. Of course she had only been running the shop for a few months, not long enough to get disillusioned with it.

Lucas was a city person all the way through. Small towns were fine for a brief visit. He was enjoying Fairhill; the town admittedly had charm, but he'd never consider living here. After the novelty wore off, he'd go nuts. No decent restaurants, except the Inn; no theater, no amenities whatsoever. No, not for him!

So why did it matter to him what Kristen's views were? He'd be leaving in a few months. He was a long time away from thinking about any kind of a permanent commitment — such as marriage. A long time.

On the other hand, he had been here for two weeks now and had seen Kristen Edwards at least twice a day. It was time to ask her out. He would do that tonight after supper. Or better yet, he'd take her out for dinner tonight.

He turned his thoughts back to the papers spread out on the desk. He had to get a report off to his father, not the most patient of men. During their phone conversation this morning, Angus Murray had let Lucas understand in no uncertain terms that he wanted some concrete plans, and he wanted them in writing.

Lucas's face subtly changed as he concentrated on the job at hand. The planes and angles sharpened and hardened, and there was no hint of the dimple now. It wouldn't have occurred to him that he was every bit as complex a person as Kristen was.

Kristen glanced critically at her dressed-up self, still wondering if she should have accepted Lucas's invitation for dinner. It certainly had been last minute, as if he'd just thought of it. Where was her pride? On the other hand, hadn't she admitted she wanted a date with him?

Yes, she had, so in that case, it would be rather stupid of her to refuse, wouldn't it? Pride or no pride? "Yes, it would," she said aloud, turning for one last look. Her silky, sea-green dress fit well, and the color was good on her. She'd used more makeup than usual, too, and the mascara brought out the length of her blond-tipped lashes. Kristen had drawn her hair back into a smooth French twist, but curly tendrils were already escaping on the sides.

Her high-heeled black sandals made her ankles ache but also made them look slender and her legs long and shapely, so she guessed the effect was worth the pain.

"All right, enough of that, get going!" she told herself impatiently. Leaving on just the small bedside lamp, she slipped a black jacket around her shoulders and shut the bedroom door behind her. She'd already told Grace good night. The older woman was reading in her room.

As she reached the stairs, she glanced down and saw Lucas waiting in the hall. As she got closer, she took in the details. A new suit — one she'd never seen before. It was blue-gray, which set off his dark coloring and blue eyes. Her nostrils flared as the scent of his cologne came to her. That was new too, a tantalizing blend of spice and musk.

That probably cost a fortune, she told herself briskly, *so it should smell good!* She smiled at him as she drew near. "I'm not late, am I?" She knew she wasn't, but felt suddenly nervous and, crazily, a little shy, even though they'd seen each other every day for two weeks now.

Lucas shook his head, smiling back, that one-sided dimple of his showing briefly. "No, right on time — but it would have been worth the wait if you were." His glance swept over her, then came back up to meet her eyes.

Kristen swallowed, willing her smile to remain steady. "I'll remind you of that the next time I'm late." Her smile froze. Why had she said that? That statement practically begged him to ask her out again.

31

Lucas's smile returned, like hers, wider this time. "You do that," he agreed, offering her his arm as he turned to open the front door.

Kristen felt relieved at his response, but the minute her fingers touched the crook of his elbow, her tension returned. Even through the thickness of his suit jacket, she could feel his warmth and electric vitality.

Brent's touch had never made her heart beat faster or her pulse race. Neither had any of the other men she'd dated. She'd told Brent she didn't want to get involved with anyone right now, but had that been the real reason? Maybe she'd just been waiting for Lucas Murray to come along.

And maybe her imagination was running away with her. She resisted the impulse to withdraw her hand and gave Lucas a quick sideways glance. Was this awareness all one-sided? How did her touch affect him? His profile looked strong and determined. *Not the kind of man to let a woman get under his skin,* she concluded, glad they'd reached his Lincoln Continental.

"I won't ask where we're going," Kristen said brightly, as Lucas started the powerful car and moved smoothly away from the curb. "I don't have to, since the Inn is the only real restaurant we have."

"Right the first time. Don't you miss having other choices?"

Kristen shot him another quick glance, feeling her tension being replaced with a touch of annoyance. She shook her head. "No. Aunt Grace and I don't eat out much, but even if we did, the Inn has good food and a varied menu." He'd probably guess the reason was financial, but so what?

"I can't figure you out, Kris. Most young women your age would be doing their best to get out of a small town like Fairhill. But you *choose* to live here."

He'd never called her Kris before. Her skin prickled at the intimate sound of her nickname spoken in his deep voice, even while she felt the need to defend her life-style. "Why not? Fairhill has no pollution, no crime to speak of, no traffic jams." Her words echoed in her mind. Hadn't she said almost the same things at lunch?

"Also no theater, no museums, no art galleries, and no restaurants — except this one." Lucas's voice sounded amused as he skillfully guided the large car into the Inn's parking lot.

"I'll admit we're short on culture, but the benefits far outweigh the drawbacks." Kristen opened her door and, biting her lip, quickly got out of the car. She didn't want to argue with Lucas over this issue.

Lucas offered her his arm again, his smile genial. "I'll concede to you this time. I want to enjoy my evening with a beautiful woman who's gotten herself all dressed up for me. Any objections?"

His abrupt about-face and his unexpected compliment destroyed Kristen's defenses. She relaxed her taut mouth into a smile, shaking her head, feeling another curl tumble down. "None. But you *did* start it, you know," she couldn't resist adding.

"Point granted. Now let's drop the subject and get on with the evening."

The moss-encrusted brick of the old building added to its appeal, as did the antique coach lanterns at the entrance. The inside had been modernized only enough to meet safety standards, Kris thought. Its charm was still intact, even to the faded Williamsburg blue of the wainscoting. Patently impressed by Lucas, the cheerful hostess led them to a snowy-clothed table in a secluded corner. Kristen felt a flash of pride that this very personable man was her escort.

The prime ribs were excellent, and the wine Lucas chose was mellow and smooth. Kristen felt her tension slowly dissolving. Lucas was a good conversationalist. He seemed to know something about almost any subject and had a ready wit that surprised her. He still didn't talk about what he was doing in Fairhill, though, she noticed, but she dismissed it. She knew from her real estate days that you couldn't talk about every business deal you were involved in.

The evening passed swiftly. When Lucas glanced at his watch, Kristen automatically did the same, amazed at how late it was. "Eleven! I'd better get home."

"Why? Do you turn back into a pumpkin at

midnight?" Lucas's dimple flashed as he grinned at her.

"No, that happens in the morning at six when I stumble down to jog before breakfast!" she shot back, returning his grin, feeling completely at ease now in his company.

Their easy talk continued during the drive home, and so Kristen wasn't prepared for the tension that abruptly gripped her again when they'd reentered the quiet house.

The night light in the hall was on, as usual. Had it always been that dim — its pale yellow glow seeming to add to the shadows instead of dispersing them? "I've enjoyed the evening, Lucas; thanks for asking me." She was too close to him, Kristen thought, moving back a step.

"I've enjoyed it too." Lucas closed the gap between them, looming over her. "I hate to see it end." His hand moved toward her, and Kristen held her breath, waiting.

His long fingers gently touched the springy softness of her hair, now half undone. "I love your hair. It's so full of life."

Kristen shrugged, trying to ignore the goose bumps marching up her arms at his touch. "It's a pain. I can never get it to do what I want." Now, why hadn't she just accepted his compliment gracefully?

His hand slid farther around and removed the remaining pins, and her hair sprang free. He ran his fingers through the silky curls, then slid them down to lightly brush the back of her neck.

Kristen couldn't control the shiver that went through her. She knew he was aware of it too. She should say good night and go upstairs to her room, but she didn't. Without conscious thought, she tilted her head up invitingly.

In the dim light, Lucas's face looked dark and strong. Even his blue eyes seemed dark and deep as they gazed into her uptilted face. His hands moved over her compellingly, bringing her forward into the circle of his arms.

It felt right to be there, held close to his strong body. The warm sureness of his firm lips against hers felt right too. Kristen returned his kiss, her heart pounding in her chest as Lucas's arms slid down to her waist.

Kristen drew in her breath, her arms going up around his neck, her fingers sliding over the thick straight hair at his nape. She felt as if she'd never been kissed before. Certainly Brent's kisses had never been like this. She didn't want to stop kissing Lucas, not for a long time. . . .

A large, heavy shape launched itself from somewhere on the stairs, landing at their feet. A loud, throaty purr started. "What th—" Lucas said.

Lucas's arms dropped, and he moved back from Kristen as Morris sidled closer, rubbing his bulky body against Lucas's ankles.

Kristen moved back too, disappointment slicing through her. She should be glad the cat had appeared just now, she told herself. She'd been responding entirely too much to a first kiss from a man she barely knew. But she didn't feel glad — she felt cheated. She shot a quick glance at Lucas.

His face wore an annoyed frown, which changed into a rueful smile as he gazed down at the cat. "Is this your Aunt Grace's idea of a chaperone?"

Kristen shook her tumbled curls, managing a small smile of her own. "Hardly. Morris just comes and goes as he pleases through the cat door in back."

"I'll keep that in mind. Do you think Morris could be bribed with a can of tuna to stay in the kitchen?"

His implication was unmistakable. There was going to be a next time. Well, she didn't have to go out with him again. But she knew she would if he asked her. And now it was time to end this scene.

"Good night, Lucas. Thanks again for a nice evening." Kristen widened her smile and turned resolutely toward the stairs.

"Good night, Kris. What do I do with this beast? He seems to want to stay with me."

His voice had lingered over her name. Kristen paused, one hand on the banister, and looked back. Morris was still wrapping himself around Lucas's ankles, his hoarse purr loud in the night-still house.

"Put him outside if you want. That'll give you a chance to get to your room and shut the door." In spite of her inner turmoil, her eyes glinted with amusement. Lucas evidently had no working knowledge of cats.

He gave her an incredulous look. "Are you kidding? No way am I faster than this creature."

She took pity on him and called the tom. He came reluctantly, and Kristen scooped him up. His large presence on the foot of her bed tonight would be welcome. Her last glimpse of Lucas showed him looking after her, an enigmatic expression on his face.

She was trying to be quiet, but when she reached her room, Grace called out from her room across the hall, "Kris, is that you?"

"Sorry, Aunt Grace," Kristen answered, "I didn't mean to wake you."

"You didn't. I'm still reading. Come on in."

Kristen opened the door, holding the cat. Once inside, she put him down. "Morris has taken a sudden yen for Lucas, and he doesn't like cats in bed with him," she explained, grinning at the older woman.

Grace grinned back, her dark-rimmed reading glasses sliding down her nose, her high-necked flannel nightgown buttoned snugly. "He's just contrary. Morris, I mean. Lucas isn't contrary, is he?"

She was plainly interested in hearing about Kristen's evening. Kristen sat down on the hand-quilted spread and obliged, hoping her unsettled state of mind wasn't obvious, and omitting an account of the kiss.

"Well, that beats TV, doesn't it? Wish I was

twenty years younger, then you wouldn't have a chance at him." Grace took off her glasses and laid her book aside, yawning. "Guess I'll turn in." In spite of her cheerful everyday words, her voice held a wistful undertone.

Kristen knew the story of Grace's blighted romance at twenty-one. She'd been tied down with her parents, both of whom were in bad health. Her fiancé wouldn't wait and had left Fairhill. Kristen's grandparents had both died within a year, leaving Grace this house.

To the young Kristen, her aunt had seemed happy and content with her life here. Now she wondered if Grace had just been putting on a good act all these years. Did the older woman still carry memories of that failed romance? Did she still wish she'd married, had a family?

Kristen shrugged, feeling ill at ease. "Me too. Well, good night, Aunt Grace."

"Good night, Kris. Let this animal out. He won't stay put long, he never does at night."

Kristen scooped up the cat again. "I'll see if I can't talk him into it." She smiled at her aunt and closed the door.

Even under the eiderdown quilt, with Morris a comforting weight on her feet, Kristen found it hard to sleep. Her mind kept going back to those moments downstairs in Lucas's arms. She'd never been so powerfully moved by a kiss before. She'd thought all the breathless descriptions in books were so much romantic nonsense.

Now she knew better. Lucas's kiss had turned

her whole world upside down. The question was, did she want that to happen? Had she and Lucas started something tonight that would grow, become real and lasting? She didn't know. She didn't even know if Lucas had been as affected by the kiss as she was. Did she even want to go out with him again, risk getting involved in another overwhelming encounter? Kristen turned over and pounded her pillow, causing Morris to complain sleepily. *All this soul-searching from one little kiss,* she derided herself. *Aren't you being a bit melodramatic?*

Maybe so, but as she lay staring at the dark ceiling, she could still feel Lucas's strong arms around her, his lips on hers.

Chapter Four

In his own room downstairs, Lucas was having trouble sleeping too. He hadn't planned to get involved seriously with Kristen or any other woman, not anytime soon. He didn't have anything against the institution; his parents' marriage had been very happy until his mother's death when he was twenty. But his life was full and busy, and he had no room in it for a serious relationship. Lucas turned over on his back in the wide bed, lacing his hands behind his head.

He liked his life to be under control, orderly and planned, stretching into the future so that he could see its shape and pattern. What had happened between him and Kristen tonight wasn't like that at all.

He couldn't be sure how much Kristen was affected, of course, but he'd be willing to swear she'd been deeply shaken too. So in spite of what he'd led her to think tonight, he'd better back off. The last thing he needed was to fall in love with a small-town girl who thought Fairhill was a great place to live and apparently planned to stay here forever.

He restlessly changed positions. Of course, she'd lived in the city for years, even had a successful career, according to Marian Dean. It was hard for him to believe she could be satisfied with this small-town life for long. A sudden twinge of guilt hit him. He should have told her tonight what he was doing here in Fairhill. Because when she did find out. . . .

"Been a long time since any man that good-looking has hit this town." Jean Howard watched out the craft shop's bay window as Lucas walked down the front steps and got into his silver-gray Lincoln Continental. "What on earth is he doing here, Kris? Surely you've found out by now with him living right here in the same house with you." She gave Kristen an arch look.

Kristen shook her head. "He just comes and goes. About all we know is that he's from Pittsburgh and has some business here in town." She felt a flash of annoyance at that acknowledgment, mixed with another emotion she hadn't put a name to.

Nothing was going the way she'd expected it to since the night Lucas had taken her to the Inn. The next morning at breakfast, Kristen had steeled herself. How would Lucas act? How would *she* act? She needn't have worried. He'd behaved as if they'd never gone out together, never exchanged that stunning kiss; he smiled and greeted her just as he had before — almost.

There was a slight reserve in his manner and eyes when their glances met. Kristen was at first surprised, then confused. When they'd parted last night, he'd as good as said he planned to ask her out again. This morning his every action told her something entirely different.

She should have felt relieved — this would give her time to decide what her feelings were for him — but she didn't. Instead, she'd felt disappointed, just as she had last night when Morris interrupted their kiss. . . .

Kristen handed Jean her change. She carefully wrapped the pillow cover she'd bought in tissue paper, then placed it in a paper bag.

Jean winked at Kristen as she took her package. "Closemouthed even on your dates, is he? Well, you don't have to tell me if you don't want to, Kris."

"There's nothing to tell, Jean. And we've gone out only once," Kristen protested to the other woman's back as she closed the door behind her. Was everyone in town gossiping about Lucas's staying here? And their one date? Her annoyance increased, overriding the other emotion.

It wasn't fair of Lucas to keep on living here, treating Grace by this time almost as if she were his aunt too, and still not telling them any more about himself than he had three weeks ago when he'd arrived. Never mind that he now treated Kristen as a casual acquaintance — that wasn't important, she assured herself.

A sudden resolve formed inside her, and she didn't stop to examine the motive behind it. She was going to find out what Lucas was doing here. Since he wouldn't tell them, she'd find out on her own. If he'd been looking at property, then Sally Randolph, Fairhill Realty's receptionist, would certainly know about it.

Grace came in with a new afghan she'd just finished blocking and pressing. "Thought I might put this one in the window. What do you think, Kris?"

Kristen turned to look at it, half her attention still on the mystery of Lucas Murray and her mixed-up feelings about him. The afghan was beautiful — several shades of gold and yellow and brown, blending with a white background. "It's gorgeous, Aunt Grace, let's do that. Here, I'll help you."

While they arranged the display, Kristen sounded Grace out to see what she thought of her plan. "I know Sally well enough to drop by and chat a little. You won't need me for a couple of hours, will you?"

Grace gave her niece a wry smile. "We should be so lucky! Go ahead, my curiosity is getting the best of me too." She didn't seem to see anything strange in Kristen's sudden decision.

"We *could* just wait until our lodger decides to tell us," Kristen said.

"But you're not going to, are you?" Grace grinned at Kristen.

"No. Wish me luck." She grinned back and left the room, pushing down a nagging inner voice telling her that her motives were not the purest.

Since the night Lucas had kissed her, Kristen's awareness of him had been greatly intensified. At breakfast and supper, the two meals he shared with them, she found her gaze straying to his large, capable hands, remembering how they'd felt on her hair, then upward to his firmly molded mouth. When her eyes collided with his, she sometimes caught a flash in their depths that made her wonder if he shared that awareness.

She no longer felt that their midnight embrace had meant anything to him. As the days had passed, it seemed more likely he'd been disappointed with their date — with *her* — and didn't want a repeat performance. Well, he didn't have to worry! She certainly didn't plan to force herself on him. Friendly, with just a touch of reserve, that's how she'd be.

Oh, stop dithering, and get on with it! Kristen admonished herself. It had been raining since last night and looked as if it would continue all day. She'd have to take the old station wagon she shared with her aunt.

Kristen came into the shop at noon from the back porch, where she'd left her umbrella and raincoat. A few drops of water sparkled in her hair, and the weather had brought color to her cheeks, but her green eyes had darkened to jade, indicating her anger, and her full lips were pressed into a thin line.

Grace looked up, a pink feather duster in her hand. "Still raining, huh? I bet when it stops it's going to get cold. Good thing the oil tank is full and we got that last load of wood in."

Kristen didn't answer for a moment, then, her voice taut with anger, she burst out, "Aunt Grace, do you know what I found out?"

"No, but I have a feeling I'm not going to like it," the older woman said dryly, dusting a glistening pint jar filled with strawberry jam.

"That's for sure! No wonder that *man*" — she spat out the word — "has kept such a low profile! He's going to ruin this town!" Kristen's anger was mixed with pain as she thought back to that first day — and how she'd instinctively trusted Lucas. So much for instincts.

Grace gave her a quick glance, then sat down in one of the comfortable armchairs beside the round table. "You might as well sit." She indicated the matching chair across the table. "What's Lucas up to that's so terrible?"

"I'm too mad to sit!" Kristen began pacing the room, her quick steps as full of tension as her stormy face. Opposite her aunt, she paused. "How could he do this to Fairhill? That *man* is going to build a shopping mall!"

Grace looked mildly surprised. "That's going to ruin the town, Kris?" she cautiously asked her furious niece.

"Of course it will! All this time, he's been looking for a site. Well, now he's found it."

"Where?" Grace prompted.

"Right smack in the middle of Main Street. Where the old buildings are now."

Grace picked up a pillow top she'd been working on and began flashing her embroidery needle in and out of the bright material. She was silent as her niece continued to pace.

Again Kristen stopped opposite her. "Well?" she demanded. "Don't you have anything to say to this — this —"

"Blasphemy?" Grace suggested. "Desecration?"

Kristen frowned, tapping her booted foot impatiently. "No, that may be a little too strong. . . ." Her head snapped up, her frown deepening as she stared at her aunt. "Aunt Grace! You're laughing at me!"

The older woman looked up, her expression changing as her gaze focused on the man standing in the half-open door from the hall, his eyes alertly taking in the scene in the shop. Grace shook her head as she moved her eyes away from Lucas, back to her niece. "No, I'm not laughing at you, honey. But I don't see that a shopping mall is so terrible a thing. Might be just what we need. Save us going all the way to Fenton's Corners."

"Aunt Grace!" Kristen's voice was horrified. "A plastic-and-glass, hermetically-sealed monstrosity sprawling all over Main Street? And those lovely old buildings gone forever?"

Grace kept her eyes on Kristen. "Kris, you know those buildings are going to be torn down anyway. The town can't afford to renovate them."

"Maybe we could drum up enough popular

support to save them," Kristen said doggedly. "If it isn't already too late to stop Lucas."

Grace sighed and put down her needle, folding the pillow top in her lap. "That idea was voted down at the last town meeting, Kris." She glanced over Kristen's shoulder.

Kristen caught her gaze and wheeled around, her eyes widening in shock at the sight of Lucas standing in the doorway. Then they narrowed in fury as she clamped her hands on her hips and glared at him. "If it isn't Mr. Entrepreneur in person. Tell me, what other little surprises do you have up your sleeve for Fairhill?"

Lucas moved a step forward. "Kristen," he began, his voice mild, "if you'll just let me explain, I'm sure I can convince you —"

Kristen moved forward a step too, until only a few feet separated them. "You won't convince me of anything. I hope your clothes are packed, because I'm giving you exactly fifteen minutes to get out of here!"

"Kristen!" Grace's voice was horrified as she hastily put her needlework on the table. "Lucas hasn't done anything to make you talk to him like that!"

"Oh, yes, he has, and if he —"

"My rent is paid for another seven weeks," Lucas interrupted, "and I've obeyed all the house rules. You can't throw me out."

Kristen glared at him. "*What* house rules?"

Lucas shrugged. "If there aren't any, I guess I can't have broken them." His face was serious as

48

he gazed steadily at her.

Baffled, Kristen stared at him. She took a step backward and folded her arms across her chest. "You surely aren't going to force yourself on people who don't want you."

Lucas glanced across at Kristen's aunt. "I haven't heard Grace say she didn't want me, and it *is* her house, I understand."

"Aunt Grace, are you going to just sit there and let him talk to me like that?"

The older woman got up. "No, I'm heading for the kitchen to fix lunch and leave you two to sort this out." She scooped up her pillow top and left the room.

Kristen stared after her for a minute, anger and confusion whirling in her mind. Finally she turned back to face Lucas. "If you have anything to say in your defense, then say it."

"All right. Do you mind if I sit down?"

Kristen shrugged. "I don't care if you stand on your head." She turned and walked stiffly to the chair her aunt had just vacated. To think that only a couple of hours ago, she'd had the crazy idea she was attracted to this man — might even be half in love with him!

Lucas sat down across from her. "Shall we try to discuss this like two adults, instead of yelling at each other?" he suggested, his voice level.

Kristen pressed her lips together. She nodded rigidly. "Certainly."

"First of all, you can't stop progress, Kris, it just isn't possible —"

49

"You call it progress to ruin a beautiful old town like Fairhill?" Kristen flared.

Lucas sighed. "Will you let me tell you what I plan to do? I'm not going to ruin the town," he said patiently. "Any construction we do will blend in structurally with existing buildings. Even the smallest towns are getting modern shopping centers now. You know that. Does it help the town that people have to go to Fenton's Corners to shop when they can't find what they need here?"

He was being so reasonable, and the last part of what he said made sense, echoing her aunt's words of a few minutes ago. She pounced on the part that didn't make sense.

"How commendable," she said icily. "Since most of the downtown buildings are at least a hundred years old, that should make for an interesting-looking mall."

The flicker of a smile touched his mouth. "I wasn't finished. Let me explain —"

Kristen decided to attack from another angle. "You can't 'explain' away the fact that when you build that mall, all the small businesses in town will go bankrupt."

Lucas's face became serious again. "People would come to the mall only to buy what they can't find elsewhere. Have you been in the town stores lately, Kris?"

"Well, naturally. You don't see me rushing off to Fenton's Corners every day, do you?" At once her conscience nagged her. She made the twenty-five-mile trip more often than she would like.

"So you're able to find everything you want and need here, then?"

He was cornering her and she didn't like it. Of course she couldn't, but she'd told herself that was a small price to pay for the other qualities Fairhill possessed. She shrugged again. "Not always," she admitted reluctantly. "But most of the time."

"Kris, you have a good business head on your shoulders. I've seen what you've done here in just a few months. You know competition doesn't hurt a business — it stimulates it to change and grow."

"What if the store owners can't afford to?" she countered. "Look at old Horace Nesbitt, for instance, and his general store."

Lucas tilted his head, his face relaxing a bit, as if he knew he had her on the run. "Yes, *look* at Horace. He's eighty-two and has run that store since he was thirty-five, when his parents left it to him. He's got more money than anyone in town and has his fingers in most of the pies. He doesn't have to change a thing. His store is a town fixture — it will always do all right."

Chagrined, Kris bit her lower lip, amazed at how much Lucas had found out about the town in just a few weeks. Her mind searched for better examples to prove her point. "How about Tom Sanders? He's been struggling for years with his shoe store and still can barely make it. His wife is a friend of Aunt Grace's, so I know that for a fact."

Lucas's gaze was steady. "Tom Sanders isn't a good businessman. If he folds, it won't be because of me."

"So what is he supposed to do?" she asked. "Just go bankrupt because your fancy mall will have half a dozen shoe stores to choose from?"

"No, he should find a partner who knows how to handle the business side of things, and get stock in that doesn't look twenty years old. Since his store caters primarily to the female trade, why not let his wife do the buying?"

Kristen opened her mouth to protest this line of reasoning and found she couldn't. What he'd said made perfect sense. Annie Sanders would love to get involved with the store — if she could talk her very old-fashioned husband into letting her.

But that still didn't mean he was right in what he was planning to do, she reminded herself. She shook her head. "It isn't that simple. It's just not that easy for a new business to get established — even in a mall. I've seen that in Baltimore. Constant turnover, empty shops, bankrupt businesses. And no matter what you say, the fact remains that an ultramodern shopping mall right smack on Main Street is too awful to even think about!"

Lucas gave her a long, enigmatic stare, then stood. "None of the projects that Murray, Incorporated, builds is 'awful.' We take pride in our work," he told her quietly. "And now, if you'll excuse me, I have a telephone call to make." He left the room, his back straight and firm.

Kristen stared after him, her feelings a mixture of anger and confusion. So he'd won. Had she really thought that all her angry protestations would stop a businessman from going ahead with a profitable project? No, of course not. After several years as a real estate broker, she knew better than that.

She got up and walked to the kitchen. Grace was just putting steaming bowls of bean soup on the table. The older woman looked up, her expression wary.

"Lucas gone?" she asked cautiously.

"Yes, Lucas is gone," Kristen clipped out, pouring herself a cup of coffee. "I know you must have heard everything we said, Aunt Grace." She wheeled, her face expressing her anger. "If he thinks I'm going to let him get away with this, he's sadly mistaken. I can't be the only one in town who hates the very idea of a shopping mall. I'm going to get up a petition to stop him."

Grace placed a tray of buttered toast on the table and sat down. "I hope you know what you're doing, Kris."

Kristen sat down across from her, resolve replacing the anger on her face. "Oh, I know what I'm doing, all right. I'm going to keep this town from being ruined."

Her aunt gave her a long look and seemed

about to speak; then she sighed and picked up her soup spoon.

Lucas opened his car door and slid inside, two deep frown lines between his eyes. He sat there for a minute, then started the powerful engine and pulled smoothly away from the curb. The next step was a call to his father. For a week now he'd been stalling, and Angus was already annoyed at his unusual indecisiveness.

He marshalled his arguments during the short drive. The alternate plan would cost much less than building a mall. Of course the return would also be less, but Fairhill was just a small-potatoes job, anyway. They'd never planned anything elaborate, the way Kristen seemed to think.

Her righteous indignation had tipped the scales toward the decision he'd just made. The mall plan was much more Murray, Incorporated's style — a fact his father would shortly be pointing out to him. He grimaced, as he anticipated Angus's angry bellow. He wouldn't even need a telephone.

At that thought, he felt his stubborn streak surfacing. He was a full partner in the business, but Angus tried to keep an iron-fisted sway over the company and had to be reminded of that fact every so often.

This was shaping up to be one of those times. Lucas wasn't going to back down on this one — for a lot of reasons. These last two weeks had been the loneliest of his life.

He'd thought he could forget Kristen if he stayed away from her. But it hadn't worked. He carried the image of her green eyes and sun-streaked hair with him wherever he went. His logical brain kept insisting he was doing the right thing not to get involved with Kristen. But that didn't help his restless nights, filled with dreams of her. Women were the ones who let their hearts rule their heads, he'd always thought.

And he still thought that, he assured himself, pulling into a parking space in front of the small white-painted brick building, its Fairhill Drug-store sign swinging in the biting wind that had come up since the rain stopped.

This had nothing to do with his heart, but he wanted to be with Kristen. He wanted to talk with her as they'd done at the Inn. He wanted to hear her laugh. He wanted to hold her in his arms and kiss her to see if he'd again feel as if he'd been struck by lightning.

He got out and closed his door, not bothering to lock it. No one locked anything here, he'd soon discovered, which was a pleasant change from Pittsburgh. *Hold it right there, bud,* he told himself, as he opened the door and smiled at Ralph Davis, the owner. Fairhill was a nice little town — but not for him.

Chapter Five

"Kristen, I know you mean well and think you're doing what's best for the town, but I'm afraid I just can't go along with signing this petition." Horace Nesbitt, his white hair framing his face like a halo, gave Kristen an apologetic smile as he handed the long sheet of paper back to her.

Kristen took it, looking resigned. "All right, I understand, Horace." She dredged up a smile from somewhere and trudged wearily across the creaking wooden planks of the old general store to the equally ancient door. After four days of canvassing the town, she'd accumulated a grand total of fourteen signatures. And they didn't really count. Six of them were from struggling store owners who were afraid of what the mall would do to their businesses. The other eight were from elderly people who were against any changes on principle.

Was that the way most of the town saw her, she wondered suddenly. Even Grace wouldn't sign it, telling Kristen she didn't want to fight her on this but couldn't agree she was doing the right thing. "We have Lucas's word that the mall won't stick out like a sore thumb," Grace had told her. "And I believe him. Lucas is a man you can trust."

"Aunt Grace, how can you say that after the way he sneaked around here and made all these plans in secret?" Kristen had said.

Grace had sighed, getting up from behind the counter in the shop to lay her hand on her niece's shoulder. "Honey, I don't think you're giving the man a fair chance. He didn't sneak around — he just didn't talk about his plans before they were finished. He was just being a good businessman."

Her aunt's words sounded very familiar to Kristen. She suddenly remembered she'd told herself that very thing about Lucas only a week or so before, and a twinge of conscience hit her, which she quickly pushed down. No reason for her to feel guilty — this was different. "Aunt Grace, can't you see he was trying to get everything all set up before the town knew what he was planning to do?"

Grace had shaken her head. "No, I don't think that's what he had in mind at all, because I believe most of the town will be in favor of this plan."

As much as she hated to admit defeat, Kristen was being forced to concede her aunt had been right. She pulled her hooded red scarf tighter around her neck as she stepped outside the store into the biting wind of the mid-October afternoon. The rain had brought a cold snap, just as Grace had predicted. They'd had the first heavy frost two nights ago, and now the blackened shrubs and flowers, even with the trees just past their peak of color, made the town look dead and cold — as depressing as her mood of failure.

She stood on the cracked old sidewalk for a minute, holding her rolled-up petition, trying to decide what to do next. She'd left the north part of town until last because it was the most sparsely settled, and she hadn't gone out into the countryside to any of the local farms yet.

"What's the use?" she muttered, as she stuck the petition into her shoulder bag, and pulled on her gloves. She had no reason to think she'd have any better luck in any of the places she hadn't yet tried.

Anyway, it was lunchtime, and she was starved as well as freezing. She might as well go home to eat while she decided what her next move would be. As she drew up in front of the white-painted frame house a few minutes later, the front door opened and Jean Howard came out the shop door, carrying a package.

Kristen closed her eyes. Of all the people she didn't want to have to deal with this morning, it was Jean, who was one of the worst gossips in town. She felt a twinge of irritation as she remembered it was Jean who'd gotten her started on this in the first place. If Jean hadn't prodded her about Lucas that morning in the shop, she might never have found out what he was doing. And she wouldn't have embarked on this quixotic enterprise.

"Kristen!" Jean called, spotting her and hurrying down the steps. "I guess you've got that petition just filled with names by now." The woman came over to the driver's side, where Kristen still sat behind the wheel.

Kristen managed a smile. "Oh, I'm not doing too badly." Thank goodness the petition was still in her bag. She didn't want Jean to see the pitifully few names.

"Is that right?" Jean asked innocently, her eyes bright with interest. "Well, that does surprise me. I didn't think you'd find a dozen people here who wouldn't welcome something like that wonderful mall plan."

She couldn't admit to Jean how close her estimation of the town's support was. "Not everyone thinks it's so wonderful," she bluffed, thinking bleakly of her fourteen signatures. And how had the news spread so fast? She'd found out about Lucas's plans herself only a few days ago.

"Everyone I've talked to does," Jean said flatly. "And I'm sorry, Kristen, as much as I like you and Grace, I can't go along with this foolishness of a petition."

"I'm not trying to force anyone to sign, Jean," Kristen said tartly. "I'm only trying to make people see that what Mr. Murray plans to do to this town will hurt it in the long run."

Jean shook her head. "I guess it takes young people like you to get all worked up about something like this, but there aren't too many young people staying in town these days, Kristen. Not enough opportunities here. This just might be a start."

Kristen was suddenly too tired and hungry and cold to argue anymore. "Everyone has the right to her own opinion, Jean," she said as pleasantly as possible. "Now, if you'll excuse me, I want to go in and have lunch."

Jean moved back a few feet. "I'll be seeing you, Kristen. Grace looked a little tired, I thought." She turned and walked to her car parked at the curb.

"Good-bye, Jean." Kristen's lips thinned at the other's woman's parting shot as she got out of her station wagon and slammed the door. She knew she shouldn't have left all the work of the shop to Grace the last few days while she circulated the petition, but she hadn't had any choice.

She looked around for Lucas's car and was relieved not to see it. He hadn't eaten a meal with them since their big argument. But she didn't know how long the reprieve would last. After all, as he'd said, his room and board were prepaid for three months, and not quite a month of that time had elapsed.

She walked tiredly up the porch steps and opened the door. "It's just me, Aunt Grace," she called as the shop bell jangled at her entry. A spicy smell wafted from the kitchen — chili, Kristen decided. That would taste wonderful on a miserable day like this. She hung up her wool jacket and scarf on the coat rack and walked through the craft room to the kitchen.

Grace was pouring milk into glasses, and she looked up. "Hi, honey. You're just in time. I was thinking I was going to have to eat alone." She put the milk jug back into the refrigerator and went to the stove.

"I'm finished for the day," Kristen said. And she was probably finished for good. She got out the box of crackers and put some on a plate. She was glad her aunt hadn't asked how she was doing. Defeat didn't come easily to her, and Grace knew it.

Grace ladled chili into a yellow ceramic bowl and put it at Kristen's place, then turned back to the stove to fill her own blue bowl. "Getting colder, isn't it?"

Kristen got the silverware out of the drawer and set it out. "Yes, I think so. It sure isn't warming up." How much longer could they keep on avoiding the subject, she wondered.

"You didn't see Lucas out there, did you? I thought he'd be here for lunch. He has been the last two days."

Kristen drew her breath in sharply. Oh, so it was only she Lucas was avoiding then, was it? Today was the first time in the last three days she'd been home for lunch. *Well, why wouldn't it be?* the reasonable part of her brain asked. *Lucas has no quarrel with Grace.* "No, I didn't see Lucas," she answered a little sharply as she seated herself.

Grace sat down across from her. "Honey, he's

been trying to keep away from you for a few days until you calm down some. But, you know, he's planning to stay here for another two months, so you aren't going to be able to avoid each other forever."

Kristen gave her aunt a quick glance. Grace did look tired, she noticed, feeling a stab of guilt. "I know that, Aunt Grace, and I'm not going to try anymore with the petition. I may be stubborn, but I do know when to quit." She shrugged and managed a small smile. "I'm sorry I've left you to do everything this week. You rest this afternoon, and I'll take over."

"Oh, fiddlesticks!" Grace protested, her hazel eyes flashing. "I'm all right — I just hate to see you feeling so upset about all this." She hesitated as if she were about to say something else, but she didn't.

"Especially when you and practically everyone in town think I'm wrong, and a little wacko on the subject," Kristen added, her voice wry.

Grace shook her head. "No, Kristen, people in this town respect you. They've known you all your life, and they know you're a sensible person. But they aren't going to go along with something they don't want to do just because of that."

Kristen nodded wearily. "I've found that out this week." She gave her aunt a straight look. "Aunt Grace, am I so completely wrong in how I feel? In trying to keep a place I love from being ruined?"

"No, of course not, Kris!" the older woman protested, reaching for a handful of crackers. "If that was what was going to happen. But I don't believe it is. You seem to have a blind spot about Lucas. You don't think he could possibly do anything that would benefit the town. I thought you two were going to hit it off for a while there too."

Kristen felt her face redden. This was the first time her aunt had referred to the one date she and Lucas had had. "I — that was a mistake. We — shouldn't have started anything." But a small voice deep in her mind asked her if she was completely sure that Lucas's subsequent rejection of her hadn't had something to do with her vehement opposition to his plans for Fairhill.

"That's between the two of you, of course," Grace said, her voice carefully neutral. "But that night when you came in, Kris, your face was lit up like a Christmas tree. You seemed more alive than I've ever seen you."

I was more alive that night, Kristen told her silently, as she quickly turned her attention to her chili. *I felt as if my whole life was opening up, that something wonderful was going to happen. But I was wrong.* "I'd rather not talk about it, Aunt Grace," she said stiffly, her head still bent to her bowl.

"Of course," Grace said after a moment. She pushed her chair back and got up. "More coffee?"

"Sure." Kristen smiled and handed her mug

over. "I'm still chilled through."

"You'd better go take a hot bath," Grace said as she refilled the mugs. "Don't want you getting flu on me. I'd never be able to manage the shop by myself," she added with a grin.

As if in answer to the conversation, the shop bell jangled loudly. "I'll go," Kristen said quickly. "I'll just take my coffee with me." She gave her aunt a wider smile and took the mug.

"Why don't you go on upstairs and take a bath, and I'll run the shop this afternoon?" Grace suggested, a worried frown between her brows. "You look awfully tired."

Kristen shook her head decisively. "So do you. I'll be fine. You go rest." She heard her aunt's resigned sigh behind her, as she hurried to the shop door.

"You're as stubborn as they come, Kristen Edwards," Grace said.

"I come by it honestly." She turned and met her aunt's eye as she opened the door, and both women grinned affectionately at each other. Kristen felt a little better as she entered the shop. She had the shop and the life she wanted to live. Lucas couldn't take *that* away from her, anyway.

She pushed the door open and blinked in surprise. Brent Allan stood at one of the long tables, fingering a sweater. "Brent — what are you doing here?" she blurted before she thought how it sounded. "I mean, I didn't know you were interested in hand-knitted sweaters."

He looked up, his pleasant face creasing into a

64

grin. He let the sweater drop from his fingers and shrugged, walking toward the small counter Kristen stood behind. "I'm not," he admitted. "I came to see you — and not about the petition, either. Dad told me you'd been by but he didn't sign it. I hope you're not upset."

"Of course not, I'm not doing this for personal reasons."

Just yesterday Kristen had been in the small café Brent and his father owned. Dave Allan had been bluff and friendly, but shook his head at her petition. "That mall won't hurt me any, Kristen," he told her frankly. "I'm doing just fine, and I expect I'll keep on that way." His friendly, pleasant face was so much like his son's. "Haven't seen you and Brent around together lately."

Kristen smiled and shrugged. "I've been real busy, Mr. Allan. You know how that is."

He grinned again and shook his head. "I guess I do, for sure. But Margaret and I always liked you. We kind of hoped that you and Brent might make a match of it someday."

Feeling embarrassed, Kristen had made some offhand, casual remark and left. Now she wondered if it had been her visit to the café that had prompted Brent's coming here now. Had his father told him about it? Could Brent have thought she'd come around looking for him?

Kristen felt distinctly uncomfortable. When she and Brent had last gone out together, several months ago, Brent made it clear he was interested in becoming much more than friends with her. Kristen had told him she didn't want to get involved with him or anyone right now. Brent took her rebuff in good temper, saying he was patient, he could wait. But he'd made it clear he wasn't planning to give up. So what did this visit mean?

He'd reached the counter now and was so close Kristen could count the freckles on his face. "I'm glad to hear that. I know I said I could wait, Kristen," he said, his voice serious. "And I have — it's been four months now since we had a date."

"But, Brent, I told you —" Kristen began.

"I know what you told me," he interrupted, "and I'm not asking you to get serious about me — even though I'd like that, of course." His grin widened. "But right now I'm willing to settle for friendship if I can't have anything else."

She stared at Brent. She didn't want to hurt him, but she didn't want to start things up again, either, when she knew it couldn't lead to anything. "That's really sweet of you, Brent, but I —"

The bell over the front door jangled again as it opened. Kristen glanced up automatically to see who it was. Lucas came through the door on a rush of cold air, pushing it closed behind him. Kristen drew her breath in sharply, her gaze riveted to his face. His eyes had instantly found hers.

They stared at each other for a long moment, neither one speaking; then Lucas said, his voice calm and totally neutral, "Hello, Kristen, Brent."

Kristen moistened her suddenly dry lips. Of course he knew by now of her failure to get the townspeople behind her, but there was no hint of triumph in his manner. She should feel grateful, she supposed. A jumble of emotions churned inside her — hurt pride, anger — and no matter how she tried to deny it, she still felt strongly attracted to him. "Hello, Lucas," she said, relieved her voice sounded cool and casual, not revealing her inner turmoil.

Brent gave her a quick glance as he waved a friendly hand at Lucas, as if gauging her reaction to the man she'd been fighting the last few days. "Hi, Lucas," he said.

"I'm going to get a couple of books," Lucas told Kristen, still in that carefully neutral voice, his face expressionless.

Kristen nodded. "Of course. You know where they are." She motioned toward the book room. She tried to push down the knowledge trying to surface — in spite of everything that had happened, she was glad to see him.

Lucas nodded too. "Yes, I know where they are." He walked through the door into the room and started looking through the selection of books.

"So, how about it, Kris?" Brent prompted her. "Can't we be friends, anyway? There's a good movie playing tonight — a comedy. You always like a good comedy."

Kristen shook her head, trying to dispel the

fog Lucas's unexpected arrival had put her into. "Wha— oh." Brent's voice and what he was saying finally penetrated. Brent was a nice man who would offer her an uncomplicated evening. Why not go out with him? It would be better than staying around here, brooding over the failure of her attempt to stop Lucas's plans.

She took a deep breath and smiled at Brent. "That sounds like fun. I haven't seen a good movie in ages." She realized her voice was a little louder than necessary, and, out of the corner of her eye, she saw Lucas's hands still on the book he was leafing through. She felt a moment of satisfaction.

"Good! Then I'll pick you up at seven?"

Brent's voice was eager and happy, and Kristen felt a twinge of compunction. Even though he'd agreed to the "only friends" condition she'd put on their going out together, she knew he was hoping that tonight would be the start of a new chance for their relationship to deepen.

Well, she'd be careful and not let things go any further than friendship. Maybe Brent needed a friend as badly as she did right now, and a little fun too.

"Yes, I'd like that, Brent. See you at seven."

"Sure thing. Good-bye, Kris." He turned and walked toward the door, pausing at the bookshop. "See you around, Lucas."

Lucas turned and nodded. "Good seeing you, Brent."

His voice sounded a little cooler than it had a

moment before, Kristen noticed. She returned Brent's wave before he closed the door behind himself; then her eyes moved back to Lucas.

One long finger was holding his place in the book he held, but his gaze was on her.

Kristen forced a smile onto her face. "You can pick out what you want and pay for them later, Lucas," she said crisply. She turned toward the kitchen, her longing for a hot bath intensified. She would ask Grace if she could watch the shop for a little while longer, after all, while she soaked the chill out of her bones.

"Kristen —" Lucas said, then hesitated.

Kristen turned, her hand on the kitchen door. For a moment she thought she saw a flash of something in Lucas's eyes that wasn't casual or unconcerned, but then almost at once it was gone — if it had ever been there. "Yes, Lucas?" she inquired coolly, but she felt her stomach quiver.

Lucas shook his head. "Nothing. I'll just look here a few more minutes." He returned his attention to his book.

Kristen, her head held high, pushed open the kitchen door. "Aunt Grace, I think I will take a hot bath if you don't mind watching the shop. But you leave those lunch dishes for me."

Grace, who was stacking the dishes in the sink, looked up and nodded. "You've got a deal. Go on, now, before you get a good chill." Her eyes searched her niece's, and Kristen knew she must have heard the exchange in the shop.

"I'm going." She gave her aunt a quick smile and left without trying to explain any of it. Maybe she shouldn't have accepted Brent's invitation — she'd have to make it very clear to him how she felt — but she'd accomplished one thing anyway. She hadn't been able to stop Lucas Murray's plans for the mall, but at least she'd made him realize that another quite personable man in Fairhill found her attractive.

She bit her lip as she walked upstairs, the moment of satisfaction fading. No matter how hard she tried to deny it, she wished it was Lucas she was going out with tonight instead of Brent.

True to his promise, Brent was only friendly during the evening they shared, but Kristen caught a few glances he sent her way. What she hadn't expected was that he had known Lucas's showing up in the shop when he was there had at least partly motivated her going out with him. She'd had no wish to hurt him, and by the time he drove her home, she was feeling embarrassed.

"Good night, Brent, thanks for asking me. It's been fun," she said. "You don't have to see me inside," she added quickly, her hand on the car-door latch.

Brent gave her one of his friendly smiles. "Of course I will. I may not have a fancy car or a lot of money, but I do have some manners." He opened his own door, and came around to let her out.

Kristen knew her face had reddened at his words. She got out and looked up at him. "Brent, I — I'm sorry if you feel that I've used you. I like you a lot, and I'd never want to do that. But as for Lucas, neither he nor his money mean anything to me!"

Brent tucked her hand in his elbow, and they walked up the steps and into the house. Once in the hall, he turned to her again, giving her a searching look. "I wish I could believe that, Kris. Then I'd think I might have a chance."

The hall light shed its dim glow over them, suddenly reminding Kristen of the night she'd gone out with Lucas. She pushed those recollections down firmly and looked up at Brent. "Well, you can believe it, it's true. But, as I told you before, I don't want to get involved with anyone right now."

Brent grinned wryly. "All right, then, will you go out with me again next week? Just as friends, of course?"

Kristen felt uncomfortable. He had neatly trapped her. How could she refuse after what she'd just said? "All right," she told him. "That sounds good."

"It sure does to me." He looked down at her in the dim light, his face shadowed.

Just as Lucas had that night. She pressed her lips together firmly. No, she wouldn't think of that. She extended her hand. "Good night, Brent. Thanks again for an enjoyable evening."

He looked at her extended hand, his smile

turning rueful as he finally enclosed it with his own. "Good night, Kris. I'll call you in a couple of days."

"All right," Kristen said, nodding, removing her hand from his and moving backward a step.

"See you." Brent gave a final wave and let himself out.

Kristen stood there for a few moments, listening to the sounds of Brent's car engine starting up. She heard a loud purr, and then Morris rubbed his large body against her ankles. She reached down to pet him, again plunged back into that evening with Lucas.

"Are you coming with me?" she asked him. He gave her another throaty purr and followed her up the stairs.

"Kris? Is that you?" Grace called out as Kristen reached the top of the steps.

"Yes, Aunt Grace," Kristen answered, feeling suddenly exhausted and hoping her aunt didn't want a rehash of this evening, as she had the other one.

"Come on in for a minute — I have something to tell you."

Even through Grace's closed door Kristen heard something in her voice that made a small frisson of unease go through her as she entered the pleasant room. Grace was sitting propped up with a book, in her usual flannel nightgown, but she looked different, somehow, Kristen thought. Her eyes looked brighter than usual.

"Brent and I had a good time; the movie was

very funny," Kristen said, sitting down on the end of the bed.

"I didn't call you in here to talk about your date with Brent Allan," Grace said, the brightness in her hazel eyes increasing. "I said I had something to tell you. We have a new boarder!"

Kristen blinked in surprise. "What are you talking about? I didn't know you planned to rent the other room."

Grace shrugged. "I didn't — but I couldn't put Angus out on the street, could I?"

Kristen felt something like alarm. Her aunt's voice had lingered on the name, as if she liked to say it. "All right, explain. Who on earth is Angus, and what's going on?"

The other woman shifted a pillow and made herself more comfortable. "Angus is Lucas's father, and he's come to stay awhile too."

Kristen stared at her, her surprise, as well as a vague feeling of apprehension, growing. "What is Lucas's father doing here?"

Grace shrugged. "He didn't exactly say, but I take it he and Lucas are having some differences of opinion about the mall plan. Anyway, he was giving Lucas some hard looks."

"I didn't see a car outside when I came in." What did that matter, Kristen asked herself, but she felt as if she were stalling for time.

"No, Lucas picked him up at the airport at Fenton's Corners. As soon as the room rental was arranged, they left again. Haven't come back yet."

Kristen got up from the bed. "I know it's your house and you can do as you please with it, but I wish you hadn't rented to Lucas's father. One Murray is bad enough to have around."

Grace patted the bed beside her. "Come on, let's talk this over. I wasn't trying to get you riled up. I just didn't see anything else to do."

Kristen paced to the window, its draperies drawn against the night, then turned to face her aunt again. "If you thought you had to be hospitable, why didn't you just let him share Lucas's room tonight? Then tomorrow he could find somewhere else to stay."

The older woman sighed. "Honey, you know there's no other place to stay in Fairhill."

"Then Lucas and his father can both go to some other town that has more amenities!" Kristen said angrily, her head turning back to the window as a car pulled up and stopped before the house.

Grace had heard it too. "I guess that's them coming back now. You're not going to start a big ruckus tonight, are you, Kris?" she asked a bit anxiously.

Kristen shook her head impatiently, listening as car doors opened and closed and two sets of footsteps walked up the outside steps and came inside. "Of course not. But I don't like it."

The steps receded down the hall, then an interior door opened and closed. Almost at once, Kristen heard a gravelly voice, muffled but plainly irritated, then Lucas's voice, its tones calmer and more reasonable, as if continuing an earlier argument.

Kristen's lip curled in annoyance as she glanced at Grace. "Don't tell me they're planning to continue their argument all night."

Grace's head was cocked as she, too, listened to the muffled voices downstairs. Then her mouth curved in a smile. "I doubt it, but I'd like to hear what they're saying, wouldn't you? I know Lucas has a strong will, but I think Angus is a match for him."

Again her aunt's voice had lingered over "Angus." Kristen's alarmed feeling returned, stronger this time. Her aunt *couldn't* be interested in Lucas's father. She remembered suddenly that the night she'd gone out with Lucas, he'd told her his father had been a widower for ten years.

Kristen let out her breath. "I'm not interested in any of it. I'm going to bed, Aunt Grace. Good night." She walked to the door.

"Good night, Kris. Don't go away mad." Grace's voice was light, but it held a plea.

Kristen relented. None of this was her aunt's fault, and she'd done only what she thought was right. She turned back around and gave Grace a tired smile. "I'm not mad at you. I'm mad at them." She pointed her thumb at the floorboards. The muffled voices could still be heard from downstairs. "I'd like to get a little sleep."

Grace pulled her pillows down, rearranging them for sleep. "I reckon we can pound the ceiling with a shoe if it gets too bad."

"I guess so. See you in the morning." Kristen left, closing the door behind her. In the hall, the voices came more clearly up the stairwell. Yes, that rougher voice was most definitely irritated, she decided. What did that mean?

A sudden hope flared inside her. If Lucas's father disagreed with him over the mall plan, then maybe that meant the older man didn't want to do anything here in Fairhill. Maybe they'd both pack up and leave in the morning, and that would be that.

She walked across the hall to her room and went inside, pushing down the other feeling that had arisen beside the hope. The thought of Lucas leaving had filled her with a sharp sense of loss. And that was just plain silly, she chided herself, firmly closing her door. Even if she still did find Lucas attractive, she didn't care for him, and he didn't care for her, so there was nothing for her to lose.

And no matter how long the arguing went on, she wouldn't pound on the ceiling. If there was any possibility that his father could talk Lucas into leaving Fairhill, she'd gladly stay awake all night. That bright-eyed look of Grace's and the way she'd said Angus's name were alarming. Kristen wanted both of the Murrays out of this house and out of Fairhill as soon as possible.

Of course she did, and she just wasn't going to let that little voice inside tell her anything different.

Kristen tiptoed downstairs in the early morning quiet. She frowned at Lucas's closed door as she passed, feeling like kicking it to wake him up too, since it was largely his and his father's fault she hadn't been able to sleep.

Their argument had lasted far into the night. Kristen had woken at intervals from a fitful doze to hear the voices still going on downstairs. She refrained from her urge to commit violence, telling herself it was worth a night's lost sleep if both the Murrays would leave Fairhill. She let herself out the front door.

The cold wind nearly took her breath away, and it made her shiver in spite of her warm fleece sweatpants and sweatshirt. She was half an hour earlier than usual this morning — it was only five-thirty — but after her restless night, she needed some extra running to wake her up enough to face the day.

By the time she came back in sight of the house an hour later, she was wide-awake but also exhausted. Panting heavily, she slowed to a fast walk for the last block, hoping Lucas's big car would be gone from its place in front of the house.

No such luck. She threw its frosted-over windows a glare, then trudged up the steps and jerked open the front door. Once inside, she removed her outer sweatshirt and hung it on the coatrack. As she turned, headed for the kitchen, Lucas's door opened and he came out, closed it behind him, and walked toward her.

As he came closer, Kristen saw he was impeccably dressed in the same blue-gray suit he'd worn for their dinner date; his blue eyes looked clear and alert, as if he'd had his full quota of sleep. She forgot her earlier vow not to say anything if the night's arguing would get the Murrays out of Fairhill. He had no right to look like that when he'd kept her up most of the night.

By the time he'd reached her, Kristen had worked up a full head of steam. Tilting her chin up, she faced him. "Good morning, Lucas. I hope *you* had a good night's sleep?" she asked him sweetly.

At least he had the decency to look chagrined. "I'm sorry if we kept you awake. But we closed the diner down, and there was no place else to go except back here."

"I can take it, but Aunt Grace is older, she needs her rest."

As if on cue, from the kitchen came the sound of Grace's full-throated laughter. Kristen's eyes widened. She hadn't even known her aunt was up yet, and it must be Angus who'd made her laugh like that. Kristen's eyes met Lucas's again, and she pressed her lips together at the look of suppressed laughter in his eyes.

He nodded gravely. "Yes, Grace sounds like she had a bad night."

Kristen whirled without answering and walked stiffly to the kitchen, with Lucas close behind her. She pushed open the door and stopped short just inside, Lucas almost running into her.

A cozy domestic scene met her eyes. An older edition of Lucas, chestnut hair grizzled with gray, sat at the table with a cup of coffee, Morris in his lap. The man was dressed in a well-fitting gray suit. Her aunt stood at the stove, presiding over a waffle iron that was giving off a mouth-watering aroma.

Blueberry waffles. Her aunt made those only for very special occasions. Kristen's mouth suddenly felt dry, and she swallowed. "Are you stuck to the floor?" Lucas whispered in her ear. "Do you need some help?"

His words — and his mouth being so close to her that his breath tickled her, making her shiver — galvanized her into action. She plastered a smile onto her face and walked across the room, Lucas behind her. "Good morning, Aunt Grace," she said and politely turned to the man at the table, who'd put down his coffee mug and now rose to meet her.

He extended his hand, smiling genially at her. "Angus Murray, and I know you have to be Kristen." His deep voice was just as gravelly in the daytime, she noted.

Automatically Kristen put out her own hand, which was engulfed in his grasp. His blue eyes were as clear as his son's. "How do you do?" Kristen's voice was as polite as her smile had been, but nothing more.

Angus seemed to sense her reserve. He let go of her hand and sat back down as Kristen moved to the stove to pour herself a mug of coffee. She gave her aunt a searching look, which Grace blandly ignored, smiling back at her.

"Any more of that coffee left?" Lucas asked from behind her, holding his own mug.

"Of course." Kristen moved quickly away to lean against a base cabinet. She wasn't going to sit down across from Angus Murray and act as if they were all in perfect agreement and this was just a social occasion.

Lucas took his coffee to the table and sat down across from his father. There was an awkward silence for a moment, then Grace flipped open the waffle iron and removed four perfectly baked waffles. "I'll divide these between you men," she said, "since you want to be on your way." She placed the waffles on a plate and set them in the middle of the table.

Lucas glanced at Kristen, still leaning against the cabinet. "Kristen, do you want some of these?"

Kristen quickly shook her head. "No, you go ahead — since you need to be on your way." She emphasized the last words, hoping they meant just that. Maybe they were going to head back to Pittsburgh this morning. Maybe in another half hour, both the Murrays would be out of their lives for good. At that thought a cold lump settled in her stomach. What was the matter with her? She wanted to see the last of Lucas. Sure, she did.

Her eyes met Lucas's. He gave her a long, thoughtful stare before lowering his gaze to the plate of waffles. "All right, then, suit yourself. These look too good to wait." He put half the waffles onto his plate and handed the rest across to Angus.

"Kris, would you make some juice?" Grace asked. "I forgot it."

"Of course," Kristen said stiffly, glad of something to do. She found orange-juice concentrate in the freezer section of the refrigerator and rummaged for a pitcher in the cabinet she'd been leaning against.

"I haven't eaten waffles like this since my wife died," Angus remarked into the silence that had again fallen. "Grace, you sure do know how to cook."

So it was Grace, already, was it? Instead of the light reply Kristen expected her aunt to make, the older woman only laughed a little self-consciously. Kristen banged the cabinet door shut. She mixed the concentrate, then poured it into four glasses. She brought two of them to the table and set them down just as her aunt brought a new serving of waffles over; Kristen noticed the warm smile Grace exchanged with Angus.

"Kris, you might as well have a couple of these," Grace said. "You look tuckered out. Run too far this morning?"

The last thing Kristen wanted was to sit down at the table with the Murray men. "Yes, I think I did," she answered, glad Grace had provided her with an excuse to leave the room. "I'm going to shower and change. It was nice meeting you,

Mr. Murray," she told Angus stiffly.

He looked up from his plate of waffles and sausage links. "It was nice meeting you too, Kristen. I hope we'll be seeing a lot more of each other."

That last remark must mean they didn't plan to leave Fairhill, after all, she decided, as she walked tiredly upstairs, her calf muscles protesting from the extra mile they'd gone this morning. The Murray men hadn't resolved whatever they were arguing about half the night. Her anger and irritation returned, along with something that felt suspiciously like gladness. No, it wasn't, she told herself. It couldn't be that at all.

Chapter Six

"So they've left?" Kristen came into the kitchen half an hour later, freshly showered and dressed in jeans and sweater. "That's a relief." She picked up a leftover waffle and idly nibbled at it.

Grace was sitting at the table having a second cup of coffee. She nodded. "Yes." She gave Kristen a quick glance. "Honey, it isn't like you to be rude to people you don't even know."

Kristen took a deep breath and put the waffle down. "If you're talking about Angus Murray, Aunt Grace, I don't have to know him — all I have to do is look at his son. They're two of a kind." Her voice was challenging and stubborn.

Grace shook her head. "It isn't like you to make prejudgments of people, either. You've always been such a fair person before."

"Do you think Lucas and his father have been fair to us, Aunt Grace?" she countered quickly. "To Fairhill?"

"I think you're taking too personal a view of what they're planning to do. Are you sure" — she hesitated, and then took a deep breath and plunged ahead — "Kristen, are you sure that some of this fighting you're doing against the mall plan isn't due to hurt pride? To the fact that

83

you and Lucas had one date, and then —"

Kristen lifted her chin. "And then Lucas dropped me like a hot potato? Sure, my pride was hurt, and maybe that was one reason I tried to find out what he was doing. But that's not why I'm fighting him now. I'm doing that because I think what he plans to do to Fairhill is terrible!"

Grace shook her head. "So you're still going to go ahead and try to get a petition against the mall plans?"

Kristen shook her head, then went to pour herself a mug of coffee. "No, Aunt Grace, I didn't say that. I told you yesterday that I wasn't going to fight a losing battle any longer."

"Then why did you act like that this morning? I've never known you to be a sore loser, either. Are you just planning to make life as miserable as possible for Angus and Lucas while they stay here in the house?"

Kristen had kept her silence as long as she could. She wheeled on her aunt. "I'd like to ask you a couple of things too, Aunt Grace," she countered. "Turnabout is fair play."

Grace gave her a wary look as if she knew what was coming. Finally she nodded. "All right. Fire away."

"First of all, are *you* taking too personal an interest in all this? Starting last night when Angus Murray arrived?" She watched her aunt closely, hoping she'd been wrong in what she thought she'd observed.

Instead, her heart sank as she saw a faint blush

appear on Grace's face and she picked up her coffee mug. She set the cup down and looked at her niece. "I guess I asked for that. Well, the truth is, Kristen, yes, I find Angus Murray a very attractive man, if that's what you're asking me."

Kristen looked at her numbly, then finally nodded. "I guess that's what I was asking, all right. I — I don't know what to say, Aunt Grace. It's not that I don't think it would be great if you" — she stumbled, then went ahead — "had a man friend. But Angus Murray? Lucas's father?"

Grace abruptly got up and took her mug to the sink. "This whole business is getting out of hand. I just said I thought Angus was an attractive man. I didn't say I was going to do anything about it or that I thought he was the slightest bit interested in me." She kept her back turned to her niece.

Kristen grasped at the straw offered her. "Maybe you're right. And I'd better go in and get the shop ready to open. I've been gone enough this week and left it all to you. And, Aunt Grace —"

The older woman turned to her inquiringly.

"I won't fight the mall plan anymore, because I've done everything I can and it hasn't worked — but that doesn't mean I like it. However, I'll do my best to be civil to the Murrays as long as they're here in town. But I hope that won't be for long."

Grace smiled at her. "All right, that sounds

good to me. A truce, then?"

Kristen nodded. "A truce. Live and let live with the Murrays. And now I'm going to give both rooms a good dusting." She pushed open the door into the craft shop and went through.

Kristen kept her word about the truce. For the next few days, Angus and Lucas Murray ate breakfast with the women, then left the house early, not returning until evening. Sometimes they ate dinner with Grace and Kristen, sometimes not.

Kristen was polite and pleasant with both men, and to her own surprise, she found it getting easier each succeeding day to maintain what had started out as only an act to keep the peace. Or had it? Her innate honesty forced her to consider the fact that somewhere deep inside, she wanted to be friends with Lucas again.

She shrugged it off. That wasn't so hard to understand — it was a lot easier dealing with people you had to see every day on a friendly basis than it would have been if they'd continued fighting. But to be honest again, she had to admit that most of the fighting had been on her side. Lucas had tried to be reasonable from the start. And she had to give him credit — not once, by word or implication, had he tried to make her feel bad about losing the petition battle to him. He was a generous winner, but then, of course, it was always easier to be generous when you had won.

She uneasily watched the growing attraction between Angus and Grace. Angus had settled into the household as if he'd lived here for years. Even Morris, who was notorious for not liking strangers, had taken to him at once. What was she worried about? she asked herself. That Grace couldn't take care of herself? That Angus would make her care for him and then leave her as her fiancé had done all those years ago? She guessed that was a large part of it.

She and Grace didn't discuss their personal feelings about the Murray men again. They both skirted a wide path around the subject, Kristen noticed, although she didn't know why it should bother her. Lucas hadn't shown any interest other than a new attempt at friendship.

She went out with Brent again, to dinner at the Inn and a movie. Again, as she had the first night, she couldn't keep from comparing this evening to the one she'd spent with Lucas. Brent came inside with her, as before, and as she began thanking him for another enjoyable evening, he gave her a wry smile.

"It's just no good, is it, Kristen?" he asked her.

"I — I don't know what you mean, Brent," she hedged.

"I mean your mind was a million miles away tonight. I might as well not have even been there."

Kristen felt embarrassed. "I'm sorry, Brent. I really did have a good time. I guess I'm not very good company these days."

"I think I know why too. It's that Murray fellow, isn't it?"

"No, of course it isn't Lucas," Kristen protested quickly. "I hardly ever even see him." In spite of her protests, she knew her face had reddened.

"Maybe that's what's wrong, then — you need to see him. I know you two have been fighting over the mall, but I saw the way you looked at him that day in the shop. You've never looked at me that way." He gave her a small smile.

"Brent, I'm sorry." Kristen placed her hand on his arm. "I never meant to hurt you, but I did tell you I didn't want to be more than friends. As for Lucas, you're way off base with him. I — I don't care about him at all." Her voice sounded unconvincing even to her.

"I wish I could believe you, but I can't. I don't think you believe it, either." He looked down at her hand on his arm, then reached out and pulled her to him. "Good-bye, Kris. None of us can help how we feel. But you'll always be my friend, anyway."

"Oh, Brent," Kristen sighed, feeling real affection for his forthright honesty and his offer of friendship. "I do like you, you know." She returned his good-bye kiss.

The front door opened suddenly, and Kristen looked up, startled, to find herself gazing into Lucas's eyes, which were now distant and cold. Self-consciously she pulled away from Brent, knowing how the scene must have looked to

Lucas. Well, what did it matter? Lucas had made it plain he wasn't interested in her, and she wasn't interested in him, either.

Brent turned to the other man with a total lack of embarrassment that Kristen envied. "Hi, Lucas. How are things going?" he asked, his voice as friendly and casual as always.

"Fine, Brent," Lucas answered briefly, his voice as cool as his eyes, Kristen noted. "How about you?"

"Can't complain too much. I was just leaving. Good night, Lucas, Kristen."

"Good night, Brent," Kristen answered, very aware that as Brent opened the door and went out, Lucas hadn't walked on to his room but remained standing in the hall behind her.

She turned to him, a tentative smile plastered to her face. "Good night, Lucas," she said and turned back around to walk upstairs. She felt Lucas's warm hand on her arm. He was so close that she could smell his cologne, the same scent he'd worn the night they went out together, and a shiver went up her spine.

"Wait, Kristen. I'd like to talk to you for a minute."

"What about?" She fought the urge to turn around and gaze into his eyes. She couldn't stand it if he saw just how attracted she felt to him.

"Will you look at me?" His voice was impatient.

Reluctantly Kristen turned back to him, and

she blinked at the intense expression she saw on his face. He looked as if the scene he'd just witnessed had upset him a great deal.

"Are you serious about Brent Allan?" he asked without preliminary remarks.

Kristen swallowed. His voice matched his expression, but she knew it couldn't mean anything. "I don't see that it's any of your business whether I am or not." Her voice was cool, though she felt far from that way inside.

His big, warm hand was still on her arm. "I'd like to make it my business," he said, his voice tight. "I've wanted to ever since that night we went out together."

Kristen's heart leaped at his completely unexpected words. She stared at him, blinking in surprise. "You — you certainly haven't been acting like that," she faltered.

Lucas grimaced. "I was too overwhelmed with my feelings to know how to deal with them for a while, so I withdrew. Then all that business of the mall came up." His voice was still tight, but now it held a trace of chagrin.

Kristen felt that turmoil of emotions begin churning around inside her again. What Lucas was saying matched her own feelings and reactions so closely she had to believe him. But that didn't mean she knew how to deal with these unexpected revelations. No matter how attracted they might feel to each other, they were still on opposite sides of an important issue. There was no getting around that fact. She pulled herself away from Lucas's grasp.

"I — I'm very tired, Lucas, I don't want to discuss any of this tonight. I'm going up to bed." She managed a small smile and tried to walk around him.

It didn't work — he blocked her way. "Does that mean you and Brent are serious, then?" His own face was as serious as she'd ever seen it; his dimple had long disappeared.

She took a deep breath, her bewilderment and confusion in her eyes. "Lucas, will you please let me by? I — I can't talk to you now!"

They stared at each other for a long, silent moment, then Lucas stepped aside. Kristen swept around him and quickly walked up the stairs. In spite of her urgent need to reach the sanctuary of her room, she stopped halfway up and glanced back down. Lucas was still standing where he'd been, looking up at her, his own bewilderment and hurt plain on his face.

Kristen hurried the rest of the way up, thankful that no light shone from under her aunt's door, that Grace wasn't awake, wanting to talk. That would have been more than she could cope with after the scenes with Brent and Lucas. She hadn't been lying when she told Lucas she was tired. She was exhausted from the confused emotions that were churning around inside her. She didn't know what that scene with Lucas meant — what it could have led to if she hadn't come upstairs when she did. But she knew she wasn't up to finding out tonight.

A sudden thought hit her. Where was Angus tonight? Why wasn't he with Lucas? And why wasn't there a light under Grace's door? She always waited up for her. Was it possible that her aunt had gone out with the elder Mr. Murray?

She knew she'd never be able to sleep now until she knew. She got ready for bed, then picked up a book and settled herself to wait it out. Less than half an hour later, she heard a car pull up in front of the house. She recognized the sound — it was the station wagon.

A couple of minutes later, the door opened, and she heard voices in the hall, low-pitched, but she recognized them too: Grace and Angus. Kristen bit her lip; yes, what she feared was true. But, she asked herself, what business was it of hers? She snapped off her bedside light and pulled the covers up as she heard her aunt quietly walking up the steps.

She didn't think the older woman wanted to rehash her evening with her niece, especially since she hadn't mentioned she was going out with Angus. Grace went on into her room and, after a few minutes, Kristen resignedly snapped her light on again. Sleep wasn't going to come easily tonight, in spite of her tiredness.

Kristen let herself into the house the next morning after her run and closed the door quietly behind her, listening. She heard sounds from the kitchen, but no voices. She gave a quick glance down the hall. Angus's and Lucas's doors were still closed. She let out her breath in relief.

She'd have a chance to talk with Aunt Grace before they came in, then. She didn't know what she was going to say, but she had to find out how her aunt felt about Angus — how far this romance, if that was what it was, had gone.

She unzipped her sweatshirt and hung it up, then walked quietly to the kitchen. Grace turned from the stove to give her a bright-eyed smile. "Good morning, Kris. Have a good run?"

Kris returned her smile, then hesitated. How was she going to bring this up? It was awkward any way she looked at it. Her aunt might very well tell her to mind her own business. She poured herself a cup of coffee, while she did her share of the breakfast chores, this morning setting the table and making the juice and toast.

Straightening a fork for the third time, Kristen decided she might as well plunge in; there was no graceful way to broach the subject. She walked back to the countertop and took out two pieces of toast. "Aunt Grace, I heard you come in last night," she said bluntly.

There was a short silence, then her aunt said, "Yes, Angus asked me to go to a late movie with him after you'd already left with Brent."

Her voice was casual, but Kristen could hear the overtones. The older woman was reminding Kristen that she wasn't interfering in her choice of men to date. Well, this was different! Kristen wasn't trying to interfere — she just wanted to protect her aunt from any heartache.

93

Kristen cleared her throat. "Aunt Grace, do you really think that you should —"

Doors slammed in the hall, male voices mingled in speech. Kristen let out her breath in irritation. She'd have to continue this talk with her aunt later.

Grace patted her shoulder. "Honey, don't get yourself in a stew over nothing. I'm old enough to know what I'm doing."

Kristen gave her a searching look as the voices came closer. This morning her aunt didn't look old at all. In fact, she looked a good ten years younger than she had before Angus came. "I love you, Aunt Grace, and I don't want you to get hurt."

Grace smiled at her niece affectionately, then squeezed Kristen's shoulder briefly. "I don't plan to get hurt," she answered.

The door from the hall opened. Kristen turned back to the toaster. "Good morning," Lucas greeted the women. Kristen threw him a quick glance as she returned the greeting. His voice had sounded different than she'd expected after what had happened last night; it seemed to hold some kind of repressed excitement. But his strong-featured face was noncommittal as he walked across the room.

She certainly couldn't say that about Angus's face. He was positively beaming. "Good morning, Grace, Kristen. Wonderful morning, isn't it?"

The cold snap was still with them, and it had

started to sleet as Kristen finished her run. She gave him a surprised look. He was pouring himself coffee, and he and Grace were exchanging smiles and glances.

She guessed he hadn't been talking about the weather. Lucas poured his own coffee and sat down at the table. During breakfast, Angus and Grace chatted with each other. Kristen and Lucas were silent, but every now and then she intercepted an exchanged glance between father and son that puzzled her. Kristen felt more uncomfortable by the second.

It was her turn to open the shop, so, thank goodness, she could escape. Finishing her breakfast quickly, she picked up her plate and put it into the sink. "If you'll excuse me," she said to the room at large.

Angus cleared his throat. "Kristen, would you wait a minute? Lucas and I have something we'd like to talk to you about."

His voice sounded different now. So that was it — this had something to do with the mall plan, she instinctively felt. Had they finally settled their differences? They must be planning to get the project started, or they wouldn't feel they needed to talk anything over with her and Grace. "Of course." She walked back to the table, giving both men a quick glance.

A knot of anger formed in her stomach at the expressions of barely held-in excitement on both their faces — as if they could hardly wait to start talking.

Angus pushed his chair back and got up, holding his coffee mug. "This may take awhile, so why don't we all have another cup of coffee?"

Kristen caught the knowing look that passed between him and Grace. Whatever was going on, her aunt already knew about it. That thought upset her even more as she picked up her aunt's cup and headed back to the stove. She didn't like this feeling of suddenly being the outsider, not after all the years of closeness she'd had with Grace.

When they were once again seated, Lucas took a sheaf of papers out of his briefcase and spread them on the table. He cleared his throat as he glanced at Kristen. "Dad and Grace already discussed this, I believe," he said, his deep voice carefully neutral, "so would you take a look at these plans, Kristen?" He pushed the papers closer to her.

Kristen shot him an angry look, the knot in her stomach hardening. She knew her aunt hadn't objected to the mall plan — neither had most of the town. But did the Murray men really think that, just because she'd stopped fighting the project, she was going to give the official plans her stamp of approval?

Lucas shook his head, as if he'd read her mind. "No, Kristen, these aren't plans for the mall. This is something else entirely. Something I think you're going to like." A small smile turned up the corners of his mouth, making his dimple flash a little.

Kristen swallowed, her eyes still riveted to his. What on earth was he talking about? He had *other* plans for Fairhill? She finally dropped her eyes and stared at the sheets of paper unseeingly for a few seconds. When her gaze cleared, she realized what she was looking at were drawings of old buildings — the old buildings downtown that were, in fact, scheduled for demolition.

She drew in her breath in surprise. These drawings didn't show the decrepit buildings as they were now. No, in these they looked as Kristen had often dreamed, wistfully, that they could once again become. No longer did their roofs have missing shingles, their porches sag, their paint peel depressingly.

Each building was redone as it must have looked when new. Or almost, anyway. She doubted if they'd ever sported the gleaming pastel colors in these drawings. Most of them had been plain white, trimmed with dark green or black, she imagined.

But how lovely they all looked, fresh and bright, their brick walks straight and even, their refurbished gingerbread trim adding the final touch. She glanced at Angus and Grace to see broad smiles on both their faces. She raised her eyes to Lucas's again, the surprise she'd felt a moment ago mingling with sudden hope. "What does this mean, Lucas?" she asked carefully.

Lucas's smile grew, turned into a grin. He tapped the topmost sheet with his long finger. "Just what it looks like, Kris. We're going to renovate the old buildings downtown, make them into shops and offices. We plan to keep them authentic too — no aluminum or vinyl siding or knocking down interior walls. Just repairs and paint."

Kristen's eyes widened, a feeling of joy beginning to spread inside her. And Lucas had called her Kris in that warm, almost caressing way. "You mean you're not going to build the mall after all?"

"Nope. Lucas finally convinced me this is a better plan," Angus put in, his gravelly voice amused. "Took a while, since we're both stubborn as a couple of mules, but those plans look pretty good, don't they?"

Kristen included Grace in her wide smile as she finally accepted this as truth, fact. She glanced down at the plans again, then back at Angus. "Good? They look wonderful! I think it's the best idea I've ever heard of!" She beamed at Lucas. "Why didn't you tell me you were considering this?"

Lucas shrugged, his grin fading a little. "After I got the idea, I wasn't at all sure I could convince Dad to go along with it."

And when had he gotten the idea? After their bitter argument that day in the shop? After she'd tried to get the townspeople behind her and failed? Had he done this, changed his original plans and then spent all this time convincing his father to go along with him, just because she'd objected to the mall?

She felt her face reddening at this thought, and derided herself for her conceit, but it wouldn't go away. The town had been enthusiastic in its support of the mall plan, his father had wanted it too, and she had no doubt it would have been at least as sound a business plan as renovating the buildings — maybe a lot more practical.

Had he done it for her? She couldn't get that idea out of her mind. A turmoil of emotions churned inside her as she looked deep into Lucas's eyes. Nothing he could have done would have made her trust him more, made her believe that he was serious about the things he'd said to her last night. It embarrassed her, it made her joyful, it scared her. If it was true, she felt suddenly as if she now owed Lucas some kind of debt, and that scared her even more.

She wet her lips. Maybe it could mean even more than that. Maybe Lucas was beginning to really like the town. She glanced up as a chair scraped, to see Lucas getting up.

"I say this calls for a celebration. What do you say we all go out to the Inn tonight for dinner?" He glanced at her, then at Angus and Grace.

"I've got a better idea," Grace put in, her voice sounding relieved and happy. "The fire hall is putting on their Halloween fund-raising dinner and dance tonight. Kris and I were planning to go anyway — would you two like to go too?"

Kristen shot a quick glance at her aunt. Was Grace's mind running along the same lines as hers? Did she, too, want to put out as many threads as possible to tie these Murray men to Fairhill?

"Sounds fine to me," Angus said. "Bet they can't cook as well as you can, Grace, but it's time you got out of the kitchen for a while." His gravelly voice held a note of concern, almost protectiveness, as he smiled at her.

Grace smiled back — a little self-consciously, Kristen noted. "You've got as much blarney as an Irishman, Angus. But I never object to eating a meal I haven't cooked, for sure."

"Neither do I. Lucas?" Kristen said, smiling at Lucas, feeling the same self-consciousness her aunt had shown.

He smiled back, his eyes searching hers for a minute. "I'm game. Halloween? Does that mean costumes?"

Kristen shrugged. "If you want. Most of the older people don't bother, but a lot of the younger ones do."

Lucas looked at his father. "What do you say, Dad? You want to dress up?"

Angus glanced at Grace. "Were you planning to wear a costume, Grace?"

Grace grinned. "Nope, hadn't even given it a thought. But I will if you will." Her voice challenged him.

"You're on. Can't let these young people think they're the only ones who can have fun."

Kristen's mouth dropped as she stared at Grace. What had happened to her aunt? She'd never have believed that *anything* could induce her to put on a costume for the dinner-dance they both attended every year. Kristen looked back at Lucas, to find his amused gaze on her. She shrugged again. "That settles it, I guess. I don't mind."

"I don't suppose there's any place in town that sells costumes?" Angus asked Grace.

"Are you kidding? Fenton's Corners doesn't have anything like that, either. But we can probably find enough stuff in the attic trunks to fix us all up."

Angus stood too. "Then that's settled. Lucas and I are going to get started on this renovation plan today. But we'll be back about five. Is that early enough?"

Grace nodded. "It doesn't start until seven."

Lucas smiled at both women. "All right, we'll see you then." He left with Angus, and Kristen stared after him, still not quite believing how everything had changed completely in the course of the last half hour.

"Well, I guess we'd better get this kitchen cleaned up, and then start looking in trunks. Want to put the 'closed' sign on the shop for a couple of hours?"

Kristen turned to her aunt and gave her a slow smile. "I guess we could do that. How long have you known about this change of plan?"

Grace smiled back, obviously relieved that Kristen wasn't going to make an issue of it. "Only since last night. Angus told me about it on the way home from the movie."

"Aunt Grace, I —" Kristen paused. "Never mind, let's get started. I'll put the sign on the door."

No, she wouldn't confide in her aunt about her mixed-up emotions. Maybe she'd been wrong, anyway. Quite likely the building renovations were a more practical plan than the mall had been. In fact, she told herself as they headed up the attic stairs a few minutes later, that must be right.

Lucas was a good businessman, and so was Angus. Neither of them would abandon a money-making plan just because of the feelings of a woman, would they? She had been caught up in the delight of the moment and had made more of it than she should. She no longer doubted that Lucas found her attractive and wanted to date her. But it was foolish of her to think it involved more than that.

Lucas wanted to enjoy himself while he was in Fairhill, and so did his father. And both she and Grace had better be careful not to expect anything more than that to come of this. They'd go to the dance and have fun, but they needed to guard their hearts until they knew more about the Murray men's intentions.

Chapter Seven

Angus opened the door of the community hall for the others to walk in ahead. Kristen shivered. The sleet had stopped, and the air was dry and cold again. Once they were all inside, Angus took a deep breath of the tantalizing aroma filling the air. "Whatever that is, I can't wait to start on it. Not as good as your cooking, though, of course, Grace," he added hastily, grinning at her lopsidedly from behind his rakish pirate's mustache, drawn on with eyebrow pencil.

Grace, her hair drawn back into a gypsy's red kerchief, laughed as she gave him an impish look. "I'll still feed you breakfast tomorrow, Angus, you don't have to keep on flattering me."

"It's not flattery. I mean every word of what I tell you," Angus answered quickly, his grin still in place but his voice serious.

Kristen stood by Lucas; her own hair was tied back in a bright kerchief and big gold hoops dangled from her ears. She glanced at Lucas, to find him assessing her thoughtfully with one eye; the other was covered, like his father's, by a black eye patch. The sweeping mustache gave him a dashing look. The pirate's garb suited him, she thought, just as it did Angus.

"Do we just sit down or wait to be told where to sit?" he asked Kristen, glancing over the crowded room filled with rectangular folding tables and chairs.

"We can sit anywhere," Kristen answered. "Nothing formal about this affair." Her eyes searched the room, hoping to find an out-of-the-way place. Her roaming glance met and locked with Jean Howard's; she was already seated at a half-empty table in the middle of the room.

Kristen let out a resigned sigh. Jean was smiling widely and beckoning to them. They might as well go sit with her. Jean would have it all over town by morning, anyway, that Kristen and Lucas were here together. And, besides, most of the townspeople were already here, she reminded herself.

"Just help yourselves, this is a family-style dinner," Jean told Angus and Lucas, her smile even wider. Jean wore a blouse and skirt, and she arched her eyebrows at Kristen and Grace. "I must say I'm surprised you bothered to get all dressed up, ladies," she said. "We mostly leave that to the kids."

"Well, now, you're as young as you feel, and tonight I feel about twenty." Angus smiled widely at Jean and reached for the serving dish in front of him. "Chicken pot pie. I haven't had this in years."

Kristen bit her lip to hide a grin as Jean quickly turned her attention to her plate. Even if she was upset about Angus and Grace, she felt a moment of satisfaction that Jean wasn't able to get ahead of Angus.

Lucas's arm, in its flowing white sleeve, brushed Kristen's as he reached for a bowl of string beans. Even that small a contact made a shiver go down her spine. She wondered if he'd ask her to dance later.

Townspeople, most of them in regular clothes, kept stopping by their table to talk. Everyone liked Angus and Lucas, Kristen saw, which surprised her a little. Like all small towns, Fairhill could be clannish, excluding outsiders. But they'd taken the Murrays right in.

"Like to come out with us on a fire sometime, Angus — Lucas?" John Andrews asked the two men genially. The chief of the small volunteer fire company, John was dressed as a hobo, one of the few older people in costume.

Both men nodded at once, without hesitating. "Sure, be glad to, John," Angus added.

"Good!" John said, his voice satisfied. "We can always use some new men. We usually don't have enough, especially during the day. Most men are off working somewhere else, since there aren't too many jobs in Fairhill. Maybe that will change a little now, huh?"

Lucas nodded again. "We hope so, John. We plan to use all local labor for the project. And then, of course, after it's finished, there'll be a lot of permanent jobs."

"That's what I heard. That sounds fine to me. Well, Kristen, you take good care of Lucas, you hear?" He winked broadly at Kristen and walked off.

Kristen felt her face burning, and she quickly turned her attention to her meal. Why had she let Grace talk her into this? Talk her into it? She hadn't objected at all, even though if she'd thought, she'd have realized it would be like this. These people had known her all her life and had teased her since she was a child.

"You heard what the man said," Lucas said in her ear, his own deep voice as teasing as John's had been. "What do you suppose he meant by that?"

Kristen took a deep breath and managed a smile, noticing that Jean was listening with a bright-eyed interested look on her face, her self-assurance restored. Kristen picked up a basket of rolls and handed it to him. "Why, seeing that you have plenty to eat, of course," she answered lightly.

Lucas took the basket and helped himself before passing it along to Angus, seated next to him. "It could also mean dancing with me after this is over," he suggested.

Kristen felt a tingle of anticipation. Well, she'd expected this, hadn't she? And she'd also wanted it, she admitted, her innate honesty surfacing. She nodded at him. "I guess it could at that."

Lucas broke open the fragrant roll and buttered it. "I'll hold you to that, Kristen."

An hour later, the tables and chairs cleared

away and the room made ready for the party, he did just that. A four-piece band was now installed at one end of the room, and it swung into a slow ballad. Lucas firmly led her onto the floor, and Kristen wasn't surprised to see Angus maneuvering Grace into the crowd of dancers too.

Lucas's warm, strong hands on her shoulders and waist made that shiver go up her spine again, stronger this time. She couldn't deny how Lucas made her feel any longer. No matter how she fought it, she was falling in love with this man. As they moved through the steps of the dance, she let herself begin to hope that something permanent could come of this.

Lucas and Angus were letting themselves be drawn into the fiber of the town — and they even seemed to want this. They could have easily found some excuse to turn down John's request to go out on a fire call. But they hadn't. Could that mean they planned to stay after their project here was finished? Maybe get involved with some of the businesses themselves, instead of merely renting the buildings? Was that possible?

"You make an enchanting gypsy, Kristen," Lucas said, his voice rumbling in her ear. "Do you think we could get out of here? Maybe go for a ride or something?"

Kristen pulled back a little and looked at him, knowing she wanted badly to go with him, to be alone with him. But she was nervous about it at the same time. "We brought only one car," she reminded him, realizing she was stalling until she made up her mind.

Lucas gave her another of those rakish grins, his dimple showing under his drawn-on mustache. "It's only about three blocks home," he said dryly. "I think Angus and Grace can manage to walk that far, don't you?"

Kristen shrugged, smiling back, feeling her heart start beating faster. "I imagine so," she admitted. "All right, let's go."

Five minutes later, Angus and Grace having agreed with alacrity to walk the short distance home, Kristen found herself seated beside Lucas in the front seat of the luxurious car. Her tenseness was back, but she ignored it, trying to relax.

"I want to talk to you, Kris, and this seems about the only place in this town we can go to have some privacy," he told her, his voice suddenly serious.

Kristen swallowed, as always feeling as if he'd caressed her when he said her nickname like that. "You're probably right, but I don't know what we have to talk about that we need privacy for." She was asking for it now. But she'd always been direct and straightforward about everything.

"Don't you?" Lucas's voice was full of significance as he glanced quickly at her. "I'd say we have quite a bit, starting with that scene I interrupted last night."

All right, she'd decided to be straightforward, so she would. No more evasions. "That wasn't what it looked like. Brent was just kissing me good-bye — not good night. I'd just told him we could never be more than friends." Her peripheral vision showed her Lucas's strong hands clenching, then relaxing on the steering wheel.

"That's the best news I've heard since all this fighting started between us." They were out in the open country now, and Lucas pulled off to the side of the road. He kept the engine running for the heater, and then turned to her. "Can I hope that decision had anything to do with me?" he asked her quietly. He'd removed the eye patch, and his eyes burned into hers intensely.

Kristen's throat felt dry as paper. She swallowed again, then nodded. "Yes, it did," she answered simply and honestly, meeting his gaze without flinching.

"Kristen. . . ." He reached for her, and blindly, instinctively, Kristen moved toward him, feeling, as his arms closed around her, as if she'd always belonged here, in this warm circle. She lifted her face to his, and his lips closed over hers, hungrily, as if he, too, had been waiting and longing for this to happen.

After the kiss ended, Kristen sat close beside him, his arm around her shoulders, feeling contented and happy. "Your decision not to build the mall has made me very happy, Lucas," she told him simply and sincerely, her lips curving in a smile.

He smiled back warmly, no trace of the teasing look now. "I'm glad. I'd hoped it would." His own voice was as honest and open as hers had been.

She didn't know how to phrase this, but she had to know. "Did you — I mean, this renovation plan will work out financially for you, won't it?" she asked awkwardly.

Lucas reached over and gently kissed the tip of her nose. "Yes, it will, or Dad would never have gone along with it; you don't have to worry about that. Actually, it's something I've always wanted to tackle, and the more I looked into it, the more exciting the idea seemed."

Kristen let out the breath she didn't even know she'd been holding. "I'm glad," she said. "I think the plan is exciting too. It will revitalize the whole town."

"I hope so. Fairhill could use some revitalizing."

His voice was still sincere, but it had taken on a slightly impatient note. Kristen felt herself stiffen at the implied criticism. Then she realized what she was doing and consciously made herself relax. No, she wasn't going to get upset about anything tonight. And she had to get over this touchiness about Fairhill. Of course the town wasn't perfect, she knew that. She guessed she'd been enjoying its sleepy peace so much after her hectic life in Baltimore the last few years that her sense of perspective had gotten a little out of whack.

She nodded against Lucas's shoulder. "Yes, you're right. Too many of the young people are leaving for good. I hope this helps."

Lucas's hand was suddenly on her chin, pulling her face around to his. His face was full of amazement. "What? Did I just hear you right? Did you actually speak a few words of criticism about your beloved town?" His eyes danced with amusement.

Kristen grinned too, feeling a little embarrassed at how vehemently she'd argued with him that day in the shop. "I guess you did. Don't faint on me."

"Oh, I'm not going to faint, Kristen Edwards. Do you know what I'm going to do?"

She just looked at him, her eyes softening, her lips curving in a smile.

"I'm going to kiss you again."

Kristen lifted her head willingly, and this kiss was even more wonderful than the first one had been. Oh, things would work out for them, she told herself, knowing now that the feelings she'd begun to have for Lucas all those weeks ago had grown, without her realizing when it had happened, into real love.

Things just had to work out, because she needed this man for always, not just for a few weeks or months. And she was daring to hope, now, that he felt the same way about her.

The cold snap ended, and the Indian summer returned, bringing crisp, cool mornings and deliciously warm afternoons.

"Isn't this wonderful? Don't you wish it could

last for months?" Kristen asked Grace the Wednesday of the next week as they ate lunch together. Since the fire-hall dance, the two women hadn't talked about their budding relationships with the Murray men. Kristen had been reticent because she felt that this new beginning with Lucas was fragile and had to be handled gently. With new insight, she guessed her aunt felt the same way about Angus.

Grace shook her head vigorously. "Nope. We wouldn't enjoy it so much if we knew it would go on for a long time. That's why these few weeks are so precious."

Kristen nodded thoughtfully. "I suppose you're right. And I must admit I'm kind of looking forward to real winter and fires in the fireplace in here."

"So am I, but I wish the fall chores were all done. We need to rake up the leaves and burn them, but until it rains, we're not going to be able to. I was talking to John Andrews's wife this morning, and she says John's real worried about a woods fire. Everything is so dry."

Kristen frowned, her aunt's words bringing back the night of the dance and John's request that the Murray men come out if they had a fire call. "Do you really think Angus and Lucas will go out if there's a fire?"

"Why not?" Grace asked, pushing back her chair. She reached for Kristen's soup bowl and stacked it on her own.

Kristen shrugged. "Oh, I don't know. I mean,

after all, they're city men, and I'm sure they've never done anything like that before."

"And you're afraid Lucas might get hurt?" Grace asked shrewdly, putting the bowls into the sink.

"No, of course not!" Kristen got up too and finished clearing the table. "I'm sure they can both take care of themselves in any situation. It's just that I wonder if they're trying to get involved in the town life."

"It sort of looks like it, doesn't it?" Grace said, running water in the sink. "Angus tickles me; sometimes he acts as if he never had a real childhood and now he's making up for it. He wants to slow down, let Lucas take over most of the running of the company."

What did that mean? Kristen wondered, a knot of tension forming in her stomach as she picked up a towel to dry the dishes her aunt washed. Was it possible that if Lucas had the sole responsibility for decision making, he might decide to spend at least some of his time here in Fairhill? Could it mean their relationship might become what she wanted it to?

The warm, dry weather continued, and three days later Kristen answered the phone just as all four of them sat down to breakfast. "It's John Andrews — he needs all the volunteers he can get — it's a woods fire."

Lucas drained his coffee cup and stood up. "I guess I'd better go put on some jeans. Dad?"

Angus, too, finished his coffee and stood. "Let's go."

Kristen and Grace watched them hurry to their rooms, and five minutes later, the two men waved hasty good-byes as they left. Kristen glanced at Grace, to see a frown between her eyes.

"I wonder if Angus should be doing this?" she asked, turning to Kristen.

Kristen was wondering the same thing about Lucas. Fire fighting could be an exhausting, hazardous job. She tried to give her aunt a reassuring smile. "He seems to be in excellent health, Aunt Grace. I wouldn't worry about it. Weren't you just telling me they could handle themselves in any situation?"

Grace gave her niece a wry smile. "I guess I was, and Angus is fit as a fiddle. But he and Lucas have never done this before." She echoed Kristen's words of a few days before.

"They'll learn in a hurry," Kristen answered lightly and began clearing the table. The situation was reversed now; she was reassuring her aunt.

"I guess I'd better call Linda Andrews. She'll probably be needing some of us to go over to the fire hall to make sandwiches and coffee if they don't get this fire under control soon."

"I'll do that," Kristen said quickly.

"We may both be involved before it's over."

Grace was right. By noon it was obvious the fire wasn't going to be subdued that easily. The

114

women closed the shop and took coffee and sandwich makings to the fire hall, where a dozen other women were already gathered with their own contributions. "I hope this means rain," Grace commented, glancing at the overcast sky.

Soon, the weary, soot-blackened fire fighters began straggling in, a few at a time, their news grim. The fire was spreading, and unless they got it under control soon or the rain came, it looked bad. It had already destroyed quite a lot of forest.

Grace and Kristen, helping to make endless pots of coffee and piles of sandwiches, didn't voice their concerns to each other, but Angus and Lucas weren't among the volunteers to come in. Finally, about four, Kristen glanced up when the outside door opened.

She let out her breath in relief when Angus and Lucas came in with a half dozen more men. Angus stopped to talk to someone. Lucas, his jeans and sweatshirt covered with soot and torn in several places, walked wearily across the big room toward the table of food. Halfway there, he looked up and saw Kristen staring at him.

He gave her a tired smile as he reached her. "I didn't expect to find you here."

"We always help if it's a woods fire that lasts very long." She heard the relief in her voice. "Are you all right?"

"Sure. Tired, but so is everyone else."

Kristen glanced toward Angus, who was now talking to Grace. He looked the same as Lucas, dirty and tired. Her aunt was smiling radiantly at him, her hand on his sooty sweatshirt. Angus was giving her a wide smile too.

She turned back to Lucas, wanting to put her arms around him, sooty clothes and all. She settled for a pat on his hand, then poured him a cup of coffee. "Here." She handed him the coffee and a sandwich.

"Thanks. I can sure use this." He took a big drink of coffee and a huge bite of the sandwich.

"Are you going back out?"

He nodded. "Yes, they still need all the help they can get. When more men come in from work, it will help some."

"Are you getting any more control over it?"

He shook his head as he finished the sandwich and reached for another. "I don't think so. All we can do is hope the rain starts soon."

Ten minutes later, they'd left again with the group they'd come in with. Grace walked over to stand beside Kristen. "Looks like they're doing all right." Her voice was full of pride.

Kristen nodded. Grace was no longer trying to conceal her growing feelings for Angus. Just as she was falling in love with Lucas, her aunt was falling for his father, Kristen thought, wondering why it didn't upset her so much now.

"Yes, I think so." Her own voice held pride, too, in Lucas, and she realized she wasn't hiding her own feelings anymore, either.

Lucas and Angus came back again a few hours later for more sandwiches and coffee, and this time they looked as if they could hardly stand. Grace's and Kristen's worried frowns followed them out the door.

About ten P.M. a hard downpour started that soon settled into a steady rain. The tired women and the current group of fire fighters let out a spontaneous cheer.

By midnight it was all over, and the exhausted men were coming back. Grace and Kristen had waited at the fire hall for Lucas and Angus, who were among the last to come in. Kristen knew Grace was as worried about Angus as she was about Lucas — but Angus was twenty-five years older. He probably shouldn't have exhausted himself like this.

When they walked through the door, both women let out simultaneous relieved breaths, then turned to each other with nervous laughs as the men gave them wide grins.

"Any more of that coffee left?" Lucas asked Kristen, wiping a sooty hand across his face and leaving a streak of black.

"You bet." She wanted to wipe off his face, tenderly. She swallowed and quickly poured him a cup, noticing Grace was doing the same for Angus. "Sandwich?"

Lucas shook his head tiredly. "Nope. I just want to go stand under a hot shower for about an hour and then go to sleep."

"Me too," Angus echoed, letting out a weary sigh.

"Angus, are you all right?" Grace didn't even

try to keep the worry out of her voice.

"Of course I am, Grace. I'm a tough old bird."

Kristen drew in her breath at the look that passed between them. It was tender and full of love. She glanced back at Lucas, realizing he'd also seen it. His expressive mouth curved into a satisfied smile. He glanced at Kristen.

"Well, aren't you going to ask if I'm all right too?" he asked her, his smile deepening.

Kristen felt herself melting in the warmth of his smile. She felt closer to Lucas than ever before. And his expression told her he felt that way toward her too. "You look great to me — except you need a shower." Her words were light, but her eyes gave him a different message.

Lucas let out an exaggerated sigh. "Can't get any sympathy even if I risk my life fighting a fire." His warm, tired smile lingered on her face.

"Of course you can," she answered breathlessly. "We're very proud of you both. Why don't you and Angus go on home? Aunt Grace and I will come along after we help clean up here." She gave him a radiant smile. She didn't know why, but tonight seemed to have been some kind of turning point in their relationship, just as it had for Grace and Angus.

The two men had plunged in and helped out in a dangerous situation and had come through with flying colors. They seemed to have actually enjoyed it — and felt a deep sense of satisfaction. That could mean, Kristen told herself as she helped her aunt and the other women clean up, that the men were interested in the town as more than just an opportunity for a money-making project.

Could it mean they planned to become a part of the town — set up offices here, maybe even run their business enterprises from here? In spite of her exhaustion and the late hour, she felt buoyed by hope. Maybe what she'd been afraid would never happen could come true. Maybe she could live in the place she loved, doing the work she wanted to do, and have the man she loved too.

She picked up the half-empty coffee can and the remains of a loaf of bread. "Ready, Aunt Grace?" As they walked out to the station wagon, she felt a deep sense of contentment. Maybe Aunt Grace could have it all too. If anyone ever deserved a second chance at love and happiness, it was her aunt.

The rain lasted for another day and broke the dry spell. Grace and Kristen, helped by Angus and Lucas, raked and burned leaves, and then the men cleaned out the gutters and helped put up the old-fashioned wooden storm windows.

They all went downtown to see the progress on the renovations, which had already started. "We're going to leave all the existing partitions we can and build around them," Lucas explained as they walked through a large frame building destined to be turned into small offices.

Kristen thoroughly approved of the renovations. The whole downtown area was going to look better than it had in years — maybe ever. And she noticed that individual businesses and houses were doing some sprucing up too, as if in response to the improving of the downtown area.

"It looks great," she told Lucas, very conscious of his nearness as they stood in front of the building. They'd been seeing a lot of each other, and their relationship was deepening with each passing day. Kristen's happiness and contentment were increasing steadily.

"Of course, we won't be able to do much more outside work until spring, once the winter sets in," Angus said, unself-consciously holding hands with Grace. "But we plan to do the interior work this winter. There's no rush."

"Yes, we're overdue for some winter right now," Grace agreed. "It's been a mild fall."

The mild weather continued until Thanksgiving eve, when it began snowing. When Grace and Kristen got up early on Thanksgiving morning to start the turkey, there was already six inches, and it was still coming down.

"Well, this will put a stop to the work for a while," Grace said, holding back the red-checked kitchen curtains to look out at the silent, white world.

"Yes," Kristen agreed, coming to stand beside her. She glanced at her aunt. They hadn't talked much about their romances lately; they'd both been caught up in day-to-day enjoyment of living, she guessed. But every now and then a nagging thought intruded. "Aunt Grace, has Angus said anything about staying here? I mean for good?"

Grace shot her a quick, surprised look. "Why, no, honey, he hasn't. But then, I hadn't expected him to. And you know it's been almost two months now. Lucas planned to stay for only three."

Kristen shrugged, feeling a little uneasy. "I know, but a lot's changed since then. I — I kind of thought that maybe he and Angus —"

"Will you look at this!" Lucas's jubilant voice came from behind her.

"I like a snowy Thanksgiving as much as Christmas," Angus said, his own voice happy and excited. "Grace, I can smell that turkey already."

"No, you can't, because I just put it in the oven ten minutes ago," Grace answered tartly, but she gave him a fond smile.

Kristen smiled at both of them, then turned to include Lucas. Her contentment was overflowing today. Both men had settled in here, into this house, as if they'd lived here all their lives. And Lucas had an air of repressed excitement about him when he looked at Kristen. It communicated itself to her, leaving her feeling breathless, as if something important were going to happen today.

Chapter Eight

The turkey came out of the oven browned to perfection, and they ate at the table before the fire in the end of the long kitchen. The whole dinner was perfect, the pumpkin pies and whipped cream filling them to repletion.

"Let's go collapse for a while," Grace suggested, after they'd made a fast cleanup of the kitchen. "I'm too full to move."

Lucas glanced at Kristen. "How long has it been since you made a snowman?" he asked her, grinning.

Kristen grinned back. "Too long. Let's go."

"Grace, we can't let those young twerps outdo us, come on!" Angus said.

Grace groaned but hung up her apron with good humor. "I guess we do need some exercise after all that eating."

"You bet we do. We'll have a contest; losers have to fix hot chocolate for all of us."

"I don't even want to think of anything like that!"

"Just wait, an hour or so of rolling snowballs will change your mind."

Kristen listened to the banter with a contented heart as she put on her heavy sweater and boots.

It was hard to believe that Lucas and Angus had been here for such a short time. They'd fit in so smoothly it seemed as if they'd been born and brought up here.

"Ready?" Lucas smiled down at her.

Kristen nodded, smiling back. "Yep. But I warn you, I roll a mean snowball!"

He raised his dark eyebrows, his dimple showing as he grinned back at her. "I thought we were making snowmen?"

"That doesn't mean we can't throw a few snowballs first, does it?" She opened the front door, and all four of them went outside into the crisp wintry afternoon.

"No, I guess not." They'd reached the front yard, and Lucas suddenly bent over and grabbed a handful of snow. Before Kristen realized what he was going to do, he'd tossed it playfully at her.

It landed on her arm, and she gave him a mock glare. "Oh, sneak attacker, huh?" She scooped up her own handful and quickly threw her hastily made snowball at him.

Lucas caught it and, laughing, flung it back toward her, but Kristen dodged it easily.

"All right, enough of that, you two children," Grace said, fond laughter in her voice. "We have work to do."

For the next hour, they rolled and shaped their creations, the heavy, moist snow perfect for the purpose. At last, as the short wintry day ended, they all stood back and admired the snowmen they'd fashioned.

"I'd say it's a tie," Angus said at last, after lengthy debate as to the finer points of each one. "We can all go make the cocoa."

Grace grinned at him. "You were right, that doesn't sound bad at all now. Maybe we can pop some corn in the fireplace too."

As they sat around the fire, lazily nibbling popcorn and sipping the hot chocolate, Kristen thought she'd never been more contented in her life. Lucas sat beside her on the hearth rug, and it all felt so right to her.

Lucas suddenly stood and pulled her up with him. "Let's go for a drive," he suggested.

Kristen glanced at him in surprise. "A drive? In this weather?"

"The roads have been plowed, and I had snow tires put on the car yesterday."

"All right." She glanced at Angus and Grace, who were sitting side by side on the settee. "Do you two want to come along?"

Both shook their heads. "No, you and Lucas go ahead. We're too lazy to move," Grace said, smiling at Angus, who nodded his agreement.

Kristen shrugged, smiling at Lucas. "Let's go, then." She felt her heart begin beating a little faster as she looked into his eyes. His expression was curiously intent as he returned her gaze, and she remembered how he'd looked that morning.

They almost had the roads to themselves on this snowy evening. Kristen glanced into lighted windows along the quiet streets as they drove out toward the countryside. People were all snug in their houses after a happy day, she thought, in this quiet, serene town.

"I always love Fairhill, but especially at this time of year," she told Lucas, her voice reflecting her contentment.

Lucas laughed. "Yes, I know what you mean. It isn't quite real, is it? It's just like a Currier and Ives print."

She frowned a little. "I guess so, but that's not what I meant." They'd seemed so in tune with each other this evening. His remark had jarred her. She smoothed out her frown, dismissing her moment of unease. She couldn't expect Lucas to share her every thought.

They'd reached the open country and drove for a few minutes in silence, then Lucas pulled off the road into a turnaround.

Kristen gave him a sideways glance, wondering why he'd stopped here. Again, she caught that intent expression on his face, and she felt her heart skip a beat.

"Kristen." He moved across the wide seat and reached for her hand, pulling her close to him.

She came willingly, nestling in contentment against his broad chest, feeling as if she could stay here forever.

"Kristen," Lucas said again, turning her to face him, "I love you very much."

"I love you too, Lucas," Kristen answered simply. They gazed deeply into each other's eyes, then Lucas kissed her, his arms holding her close against him.

Then he moved back a little and fumbled in the pocket of his jacket. He pulled out a small box and opened it.

Kristen drew in her breath as Lucas worked the ring free of its velvet cushion and held it out to her, a question on his face. The square-cut diamond, flanked by emeralds, reflected in the dome light, sparkling and shining in the dimness of the car. Her eyes wide, she could only stare at him.

Lucas smiled. "May I put this on your finger, Kristen?" he asked gently. "I've been wanting to do this for weeks now."

Kristen moistened her dry lips and nodded, not trusting herself to speak. She held out her hand and saw it was trembling.

Lucas steadied it and slipped the ring on her finger, then drew her toward him for another long, tender kiss.

When they drew apart, Kristen held out her hand, looking at the ring in wonder. "It's so beautiful — I didn't expect this, Lucas."

He quirked an eyebrow, his arm still around her shoulder. "You didn't? I thought I'd been making my intentions pretty clear lately."

She smiled tremulously. "Well, you never said anything. . . ."

"I wanted everything to be just right," he answered gently. "I special ordered the ring from New York, and there were a few other things I had to see to."

Kristen didn't understand what he meant, but

she didn't really care. She was too full of love and happiness for anything else to matter.

Lucas was pulling away from her again. "Excuse me." He leaned across her, opened the glove compartment, and drew out a rolled sheaf of papers. He unrolled them and smoothed them out, spreading them across both their laps.

Kristen shot him an inquiring look. "You look as if you just can't wait to show me this, whatever it is." She smiled at him fondly.

He grinned back happily. "I can't. I've been working on these for weeks."

She turned her attention back to the papers and looked closely. They were building plans, scale drawings, she saw, surprised. Lucas moved the bottom paper up to the top, revealing a full-color sketch that reminded her of the ones she'd seen for the old buildings downtown.

But this was only one house, a beautifully worked-out Victorian replica, complete even to the carefully detailed gingerbread trim and the stained-glass panels in the front door. She glanced up at Lucas again. "I don't understand — what is this? Something else you're going to build?"

Lucas shook his head in mock despair. "You can be awfully slow sometimes, Kris. Yes, it certainly is something I plan to build." His long fingers moved to the sheet, pointing out some writing in the corner she hadn't noticed.

" 'Our dream house — Kristen's and mine,' " Kristen read aloud. She swallowed as tears came to her eyes. She turned back to Lucas, her eyes shining. "Oh, Lucas, how beautiful! How did you know that's exactly the kind of house I'd want to live in?"

He traced his hand along her cheek. "It wasn't all that hard, since you love Grace's house so much."

She felt as if her heart would burst with happiness. She looked at the sketch of the beautiful house again, then back at Lucas. "It's wonderful. And I know the perfect site for it too," she told him excitedly. "There's a two-acre lot for sale at the north end of town that has a lot of gorgeous old walnut and maple trees."

She gave him a radiant smile, which slowly faded as she saw the frown on his face, his suddenly altered expression. "What's wrong?" she asked him hesitantly. "Do you already have a site picked out?"

Lucas looked at her for another long moment, then nodded. "Yes, I do," he finally said. "I've owned a five-acre plot for several years that I thought would be just right."

She stared at him in bewilderment. "Several years? But — how could you have owned it that long? I thought you'd never been to Fairhill before."

Lucas nodded heavily. "I haven't been. This plot is on the outskirts of Pittsburgh."

"Pittsburgh?" Kristen glanced from the sketch back to him. Slowly she realized what he meant, and the look of happiness faded from her face.

"You've planned to go back to Pittsburgh all along, then?" she asked him numbly.

Lucas nodded again, a hint of impatience in his expression. "Yes, of course I have. What else did you think I had in mind?"

Her heart felt like a lead weight in her chest now. She stared at him steadily. "I had the insane idea that you were planning to stay in Fairhill."

His expression grew incredulous. "Stay in Fairhill? How on earth could I do that? I have a business to run."

She shrugged. "Crazy, wasn't it? You seemed to be getting to like the town a lot, becoming involved in it. I — I thought you could set up your headquarters here."

Lucas shook his head as if he couldn't believe his ears. "Well, sure, I do like this little place, Kristen. It's pretty and peaceful. But I never considered living here. I thought —"

The beautiful ring on Kristen's finger seemed to have gotten heavier in the last few moments. It felt like a lead weight now. "So without even consulting me, you just went ahead and made all these plans. Didn't you ever stop to think that I might not want to leave Fairhill?" Her tone and her words were cool.

Lucas's firm jaw had tightened as she talked. "I thought that for once you would be sensible."

Her eyes flashed green fire at him. "Sensible? Does that mean you expect me to leave the only place I've ever wanted to live, and move to a city

129

again? When I've told you how much I hate city life!"

He let out a sigh of exasperation. "You have to be the most stubborn person I've ever come across. I've got a business to run. Come out of your never-never land into the real world!"

Kristen swallowed, blinking back the tears that again threatened to overflow. But these tears were far different from the ones of a few minutes ago. She reached down, stripped off the ring, and thrust it at him. "This has to be the shortest engagement on record, but I guess it's a good thing we found out now just how incompatible we really are."

Lucas automatically took the ring, then pushed it roughly into his jacket pocket. His face was set in the same hard lines as Kristen's. "I guess it is." He turned abruptly away from her and started the car.

They didn't say a word to each other all the way back to Fairhill. When Lucas parked in front of the house, Kristen opened the car door before he could say anything and walked quickly into the house. She could hear Angus's and Grace's voices coming from the kitchen and quietly hurried upstairs before her aunt had a chance to call to her. She couldn't talk to anyone now.

She heard Lucas come in but didn't stop until she was safe in her room, with her door securely closed. She could let the tears come now; no one could see them. It seemed impossible she'd reached the pinnacle of happiness and then been plunged down into such hopeless despair in only a few minutes.

How could she have been so mistaken about Lucas's plans? But how could he have done this to her? Why, they really hadn't known each other at all. Both of them had gone blindly along making their own plans — plans that could never be reconciled with each other. She'd been a fool to think that a successful businessman like Lucas could ever have considered living here in Fairhill! She could see that now.

But on the other hand, Lucas had known from the beginning that she never wanted to live in a city again. She'd made that crystal clear. And he'd ignored it, gone ahead and drawn up those house plans without even consulting her! She was certainly lucky that she'd discovered what an insensitive, thoughtless man he was now, before they were married.

But she didn't feel lucky, she thought dully as she lay across her bed, tears running down her face and falling onto the quilt. She felt as if she'd never be happy again.

For the first time in years, Kristen overslept the next morning. When she finally came downstairs at eight she found Grace in the kitchen alone, kneading bread dough. One look at her aunt's anxious face told Kristen that she knew what had happened between her and Lucas.

She forced a smile. "Good morning, Aunt

Grace. I'm sorry I overslept. You should have called me."

"I thought you needed the sleep — after last night."

So Lucas had told Angus about their breakup. Kristen walked over to the stove and poured herself a cup of coffee. She glanced at Grace, to find the other woman giving her a worried look. "Aunt Grace, I don't want to talk about Lucas right now."

Grace sighed, punching the dough and then rolling it over. "All right, but are you sure you did the right thing?"

Kristen added milk to her coffee and took a long sip. "Yes, I'm sure. Now let's just drop it, okay?"

Grace was silent as she finished kneading and put the dough in a greased bowl to rise. Kristen finished her coffee and decided to skip breakfast. She wasn't hungry this morning. "I'll open the shop," she said, pouring herself another cup of coffee to take in with her.

"Fine," Grace said, "I need to do some long-overdue housecleaning."

The shop had a lot of customers, starting to look for Christmas gifts, for which Kristen was grateful. She didn't want to have time to think about what had happened last night. She'd cried herself out, and she couldn't face any more pain right now.

Lucas and Angus didn't come home for lunch. Kristen ate a quick bowl of soup and a sandwich and went back to the shop, which kept her busy all afternoon.

By five, when the last customer finally left, she was exhausted, but at least she hadn't had time to brood. That was something to be thankful for, she guessed. Angus and Lucas had come in a few minutes earlier while she'd been busy with a customer. They'd spoken and gone on to their rooms. Lucas's greeting had been cool and polite.

Now she heard a door opening and footsteps coming down the hall. She listened, a hard knot forming in her stomach. Lucas appeared in the doorway, holding his suitcases. He looked at her, a long searching look, and Kristen could only stare back rigidly. She heard Grace come into the craft shop and stop behind her.

Finally Lucas turned away. "Good-bye, Grace," he said, his voice softening as he smiled at the older woman. "I've enjoyed living here these few months."

Grace looked deeply distressed as she walked a few steps toward him, then stopped. "Are you leaving Fairhill, Lucas?"

He nodded. "Yes. Dad is going to stay on for a while longer. He can do everything that needs to be done. And I believe he has some very personal reasons for staying on too." He gave her another fond smile, belied by his rigid posture.

Grace looked from him to Kristen. "Can't you two talk this out?" she pleaded.

Lucas shook his head decisively. "No, I'm

afraid not, Grace. There's really nothing to talk about. I'll be in touch with Dad. Maybe he'll have something to tell me in a few days," he added significantly.

Kristen watched the blush spread over her aunt's face and knew what Lucas was hinting at. Angus was going to ask Grace to marry him.

"I wish you wouldn't leave like this, Lucas," Grace said, but her voice was resigned.

Lucas shrugged, then turned and looked at Kristen. "Good-bye, Kristen," he said. His voice sounded final.

Kristen's throat felt too dry to form any words. She watched numbly as he turned and walked to the door and opened it. She heard his footsteps going down the steps and out to the Lincoln. In a moment the powerful engine roared to life, and after a few minutes' warming up, the car pulled away. She listened until the sound faded in the distance.

"Well, I guess that's that." She tried to smile, to make her voice casual and unconcerned, but she heard the wobble in it and could feel the tears behind her eyelids. She blinked and swallowed.

"Oh, Kristen! I don't know what to say." Grace's voice was unhappy, strained. She walked toward her niece.

Kristen wheeled and walked out from behind the counter, over to the window. She couldn't bear her aunt's sympathy now. She stared unseeingly out the frosted-over panes.

In a moment she felt Grace's hand on her shoulder. "Kris, if there's anything I can do, you know I'm always there for you."

Kristen didn't turn. She didn't want her aunt to see the tears that were running down her face. "I know that, Aunt Grace. Thanks," she managed to say.

"I'm going to put the kettle on," Grace said and left the room. Coffee and tea, the universal panaceas for all troubles. It would take more than tea or coffee to fix this problem. Nothing could fix it, she thought bleakly, swiping at the tears with the back of her hand.

She heard Angus's door open again, and then in a moment, she heard him talking in low tones to her aunt. His rough voice sounded worried and concerned too, she thought.

She'd missed her run this morning, and she suddenly badly needed it. It was late, but if she got caught out in the dark, so what? Fairhill's streets were safe anytime — oh, yes, she knew that. Fairhill was safe, clean, quiet, and serene — the place she wanted to live her life out in.

But without Lucas here, she might as well be back in Baltimore. Or Pittsburgh. She went quickly upstairs to her room and changed into her running clothes. She could still hear the rumble of Angus's voice, mingling with her aunt's softer tones.

"I'm going running, Aunt Grace," she called, then let herself out the front door. There was a bare space in the snow along the curb where

Lucas's car had sat, and tire prints led out in a curve where he'd pulled into the street. A stab of anguish hit Kristen as she looked at the tracks disappearing into the distance.

She pressed her lips together and began walking rapidly down the snowy sidewalk to warm up. It was over, and she might as well forget it. Lucas was gone. The thought echoed in her mind as she gradually accelerated her walk to a jog, then a run.

Her life would never be the same again.

Chapter Nine

Lucas concentrated on his driving, glad of the snowy, treacherous roads. At least he wouldn't have to think about what had happened with Kristen. He should be grateful he'd found out now just how unreasonable she could be. Of course he'd known that already, after the ruckus over the mall. But that episode had also shown him she was sensible too. She wouldn't go on fighting just for the sake of fighting.

That was why he hadn't given much thought to how his house plans would strike her. He'd just assumed she'd understand why he couldn't settle down in Fairhill. Not with a business like Murray, Incorporated, to run. After all, she'd been a businesswoman too. Well, she still was, of course, but the shop couldn't compare with the real estate career she'd abandoned.

A stop sign loomed ahead, and Lucas began braking carefully. The roads were plowed but still slippery. Angus had tried to talk him into staying, but he wouldn't listen, as his pride had started taking over by then. He'd bent over backward to placate Kristen that first time; why, he'd even spent days talking his father into changing their plans, giving up the mall idea.

All for her. Well, mostly, anyway. The renovations were a sound idea, maybe even better than the mall plan. But, still, he'd done everything he could to make Kristen happy. And that hadn't been enough.

Yes, he was lucky he'd found out now just how unreasonable and stubborn she could be. He wouldn't want a marriage that was one constant battle over everything that came up.

He banged his clenched fist on the steering wheel. "So I'll just forget Kristen Edwards and get on with my life," he muttered as he reached the outskirts of Fairhill and made the turn onto the interstate that would take him back to Pittsburgh.

"Kris, I need to talk to you."

Grace came into the shop where Kristen sat behind the counter. A week had passed since Lucas's departure from Fairhill. Kristen felt as if it had been a year.

She gave her aunt what she hoped was a carefree smile. "Sure, Aunt Grace." Grace's face wore an expression of suppressed excitement, as if she were bursting to talk, but she looked a little uneasy too.

Grace settled herself into the wing chair and picked up her current piece of crocheting. "Honey, you know how Angus and I feel about each other," she began, then lowered her head to her work for a minute. Finally she grimaced and dropped it back into its basket. She took a visibly deep breath.

Kristen gave her another smile and swallowed. "Aunt Grace, you don't have to be nervous about telling me. Angus has asked you to marry him, hasn't he?"

Some of the tension left the older woman's face. She nodded. "Yes, he has, Kris, and I've said yes." A radiant smile spread over her face for a moment, then she bit her lip.

Kris came out from behind the counter and walked over to her aunt, then hugged her warmly. "Aunt Grace, I'm so happy for you. I really am. I like Angus a lot. I think you'll be very happy."

The remaining tension left her face at Kristen's reassuring words. "Oh, Kristen, I'm so glad! I've been afraid that —"

Kristen gave her a straight look. "That since Lucas and I broke up, I wouldn't want you to marry Angus. Of course I don't feel that way. My quarrel with Lucas has nothing to do with his father."

Grace returned her niece's level look. "Are you sure you did the right thing, Kris? There aren't too many men around like Angus and Lucas."

Kristen moved away a few feet. "I know that, Aunt Grace. I didn't break off with Lucas over some little issue. It was about the most basic thing there is, I guess — the kind of life we want to live."

"Did you two try to talk it out, come to some sort of compromise?"

Kristen shook her head. "No, Aunt Grace. Lucas never even thought of what I wanted. He went ahead and drew up those house plans when he knows how much I hate city life. He didn't even consult me. Does that sound like a man who wants to compromise?"

Grace sighed and picked up her crocheting again. "I guess not, but you can be mighty stubborn too, Kris."

"Those years in Baltimore were enough to finish me off with big-city life forever, Aunt Grace. That's why I came back here. I have no intention of moving back to a city. Not for any reason."

"Several acres in the suburbs isn't exactly the same as living in the middle of a city, like you did."

"It isn't just that, Aunt Grace. I have my own life here. I like running this shop. I love Fairhill. Lucas didn't even bother discussing it with me. He just assumed that he could arrange our lives any way he wanted to and that I'd go along with him."

Grace gave her a shrewd look, and then her mouth turned up in a tiny smile. "Honey, are you sure you're not letting principles and pride get in the way here? Instead of listening to your feelings?"

Kristen gave her a stricken look and swallowed hard. Her aunt had hit a sore spot. *Was* that what she'd done? No! It wasn't. She'd just been sensible. "I — you can't let your emotions decide your life. You have to listen to your head."

Grace nodded, putting down her crocheting again. "Of course you do. But sometimes your head can lead you on a wrong course too, just like your heart can." She sighed. "All I know is that you two care for each other. The Murray men have a lot of pride too, you know. Sounds to me like you're both being stubborn."

Kristen shook her head. "No, just realistic. We both know it could never work out."

Grace gave her niece a rueful smile. "All right, I'll let you alone and go on with the next thing I need to talk about. Angus wants to get married right away — before Christmas, in fact. And we've decided we'd like to have a small wedding here in the house."

Kristen took a deep breath, then smiled. No matter how she felt, she wouldn't spoil her aunt's big moment. "That's great, Aunt Grace! But it means we're going to be busy, doesn't it?"

Grace nodded. "We plan on keeping things as simple as possible. We want Lucas to come, of course. We'd like you both to stand up with us."

Kristen sucked in her breath. "I'm willing, but I don't know how Lucas will feel."

"Angus has already asked him," Grace said quickly. "He said the same thing."

Kristen wet her lips as hope flared wildly inside her. Could Lucas's acceptance mean that he, too, regretted their quarrel? That he wanted to try to work something out? She quickly doused her sudden hope. There was nothing to work out, and she knew it. It was senseless to try.

"Well, looks like it's all settled, then."

Grace nodded. "I guess so. There's just one other thing, Kris." She hesitated, as if unsure how to approach this next subject. "Angus wants to travel, and I'd enjoy that too. We plan to take a six-month trip to Europe. But I hate to leave you with all the running of the shop. Now that business is picking up, it really would be too much for you."

"Don't you worry about that," Kristen said swiftly, giving her aunt a reassuring smile. "I've known this was coming, and I've been thinking about it. I'm sure Thelma Morgan would be willing to work here part-time. She often stays after she brings something in, and helps me sort books. She's hinted that she'd like to work here."

Grace's face cleared, and a wide smile broke out on it. "That does relieve my mind. But are you sure you want to stay on here? Angus and I haven't made any hard-and-fast plans for the future yet. I don't want to ever sell this house, and of course you're welcome to live here as long as you like, and to run the shop. But are you sure you want to? Are you missing your real estate career at all by now?"

Kristen shook her head vigorously. "No, I've never for one minute missed that, and I still love Fairhill. I'd rather stay on here, Aunt Grace. And I'll see if Thelma can start work right away."

Grace nodded. "All right, then that's settled.

And, honey, Angus and I both hope that you and Lucas can work out your problems when he comes for the wedding."

Kristen shook her head. "Aunt Grace, you never give up, do you? Even when it's a lost cause."

Kristen threw herself feverishly into the wedding preparations, in spite of her aunt's protestations that she and Angus didn't want a big, elaborate affair.

"Elaborate, no; beautiful, yes," Kristen insisted as she cleaned and polished the small sitting room downstairs. They seldom used it now, preferring the coziness of the big comfortable kitchen.

"But there's no place else for a wedding, is there?" Grace had said as they looked it over.

"No, unless you want to be really informal and have it in the kitchen," Kristen answered dryly.

"I love my kitchen, but maybe that's going a little too far," Grace admitted.

"I think you're right. Now, how about flowers? Since it's going to be almost a Christmas wedding, do you want to have poinsettias, holly — mistletoe?" She tried to keep her voice light, but no matter how happy she was for Grace and Angus — and she truly felt that way — the wedding preparations were tearing her apart emotionally. *This could just as well have been for you and Lucas too,* her mind relentlessly reminded her.

Grace nodded, her eyes brightening. "Yes, I

think that would be nice, don't you? So cheerful and warm."

"I agree. And it won't be hard to find those flowers this time of year — even in Fairhill."

"That's true. I hadn't thought of that angle."

Now, a week before the wedding date, everything was done. Not only the sitting room but the entire house shone and sparkled, Christmas decorations brightening its large rooms.

"Have you seen to Lucas's room yet?" Grace asked Kristen that morning after breakfast. Angus had eaten with them, as usual, then left to go downtown to check on the interior renovations that were proceeding well.

A pang went through Kristen at her aunt's words. She'd been avoiding the fact that there was one room left uncleaned and untidied. "No, I haven't," she answered.

"Honey, would you rather I did?" Grace asked tactfully. "If it bothers you —"

Kristen shook her head quickly. "No, don't be silly. Of course I'll do it. I just haven't gotten around to it yet." That wasn't the real reason, and she figured her aunt probably knew it. She'd been putting off going into the room Lucas had occupied, wary of the emotions that would waken in her.

"All right, if you're sure," Grace said. "Lucas is going to stay overnight before the wedding, you know."

The news made her heart beat faster, anticipation leaping through her, in spite of everything

144

that had happened. That meant they'd have a little time together. . . .

"I'd better get cracking on Lucas's room, then," she said, smiling at her aunt.

Grace returned the smile fondly. "Honey, think positively. I just have a feeling everything is going to work out for you two. I know you love each other."

"Unfortunately, love doesn't solve all problems." Kristen gathered up clean sheets and her cleaning supplies and let herself into Lucas's room for the first time since he'd left. She stood just inside the door for a moment, looking around. She inhaled deeply. The room still smelled like him; he'd left behind the distinctive, spicy scent of his after-shave and soap. . . .

His bed was neatly made, as usual. He'd done that every morning. Even his hurried departure hadn't made him forget his organized ways, she noted. The only sign that the room had recently been occupied was a dresser drawer left ajar.

She crossed the room and started to close the drawer, but it jammed on something. She wiggled it a little, and when that didn't loosen it, she pulled it all the way open. Some folded sheets of paper were wedged in the top, she saw, and she carefully eased them out.

It looked like plans for the downtown buildings, she noted, glancing at the sheets. Architectural drawings. Then, as she looked closer, she drew in her breath. These weren't plans for the downtown buildings. They were the house plans

Lucas had shown her that night — the ones that had precipitated their breakup.

Her hands clenched on the papers as despair went through her. She felt like tearing them into pieces and throwing them in the wastebasket. Then her hands stilled and she read again, in Lucas's firm, clear handwriting, *Our dream house — Kristen's and mine.* Her heart turned over inside her. A man didn't design a house for a woman unless he truly loved her. She carefully refolded the papers and put them back into the drawer.

She changed the sheets, then plugged in the vacuum and mechanically cleaned the room, trying to blot out the images of Lucas that seeing his handwriting on the plans had evoked: Lucas at the fire-hall dance, his pirate's garb making him look so handsome. Lucas coming in from fighting the woods fire, sooty and exhausted. She and Lucas throwing snowballs on Thanksgiving, making a snowman. And finally the last scene of all: Lucas, his face and voice tender, gently slipping the ring on her finger. . . .

Quickly she gathered up her cleaning supplies and left the room, tears blinding her. Lucas was the only man she'd ever love, she knew in that moment. She thought he still loved her too. And it made no difference at all. They could never make it work between them.

Lucas felt his anticipation growing the nearer he got to Fairhill. When he finally turned off the

146

interstate onto the blacktopped highway leading into the town, his heart was beating faster, his pulse racing.

He looked fondly at the landmarks that had become familiar to him during the short time he'd lived there. He hadn't missed them, of course; Pittsburgh still suited him fine, but just the same, because this was the place where Kristen lived, it meant something special to him.

Angus had hinted during their frequent calls the last few weeks that Kristen missed him, that he was sure she was sorry they'd quarreled.

Well, he was too. No other woman looked good to him now. All he could think of was a small woman with brownish-blond hair and green eyes that darkened to jade when she was angry — which was the way he'd last seen her, he reminded himself, and for all he knew, the way she still was. She was stubborn and determined; that he knew for sure from the way she'd fought the mall plan.

He didn't know what to expect when he parked the Lincoln in front of Grace's familiar house, walked up the steps, opened the door with the stained-glass panels. But he still loved and wanted Kristen Edwards. He wanted to build that house for her on the acreage in the Pittsburgh suburbs, which he'd gone out and looked at a dozen times in the last two weeks.

And he was willing to forgive and forget that stupid quarrel they'd had. He was going to walk up those steps and open that door and try to make that stubborn woman see they belonged together.

Kristen heard the bell on the door jingle as she finished up the supper dishes. Grace and Angus had gone off somewhere, she wasn't quite sure where, and they shouldn't be back yet. And the shop had the "closed" sign out — she thought.

Maybe it didn't, but she had far too much yet to do to bother with another customer. Maybe it was just Thelma. Halfway through the craft-room doorway, she stopped, her heart thudding in her chest at the sight of Lucas standing in the hall.

All the things she'd told herself and all the reasons it could never work for them fled her mind at that first sight of him. He looked so wonderful, his chestnut hair rumpled, those in-credible blue eyes giving her a searching look, a tentative smile on his face.

"Hello, Kristen," he said simply, walking into the room a few feet and then pausing, as if wait-ing for her to make the next move.

Kristen took a deep breath, trying to slow her erratic heartbeat. She steeled herself against the turmoil of feelings Lucas was arousing inside her. She couldn't let him know how he affected her, she reminded herself desperately. It could never work; there was no use starting anything up again.

"Hello, Lucas," she said carefully, walking to-ward him, her small smile as polite as her words.

"Come in, won't you? How have you been? Your room's ready for you." That sounded right, she assured herself, just the way she'd speak to any casual acquaintance.

Lucas stood where he was for a moment, searching her eyes, her face, as if he could penetrate the mask she had arranged there. "I've been fine, Kristen. I don't have to ask how you've been. You look wonderful."

Her throat felt so dry she could hardly swallow. She ignored his words, his warm voice. "Angus and Grace are out somewhere, but they should be back soon. I — I guess you want to take that to your room." She gestured to his small suitcase.

Lucas set the suitcase down and took a few steps toward her, his face intent. "Kristen, stop acting as if you've just met me. We have to talk."

She backed up a little. If he kept this up, she wouldn't be able to hold on to her resolutions, no matter how right and sensible she knew they were. She heard a car stop outside. Recognizing it as the station wagon, she breathed a sigh of profound relief. Thank goodness, Angus and Grace were back. She had to get away from Lucas before she weakened. She brightened her smile. "There they are now."

Lucas gave her a frustrated look just as Grace and Angus came in, their faces happy and excited, eager and welcoming. Angus and Lucas shook hands and clapped each other on the shoulders, and Grace hugged Lucas, her face radiant.

"Come on in and have some coffee!" Grace said, her voice happy and excited too. "Kristen," she questioned, turning to her niece, "there is some left, isn't there, from supper?" Then she seemed to notice her niece's strained expression. Some of the excitement faded from her face.

Kristen felt stricken. The last thing she wanted to do was spoil her aunt's happiness. She forced a wide smile onto her face. "If not, I'll make some." She hurried out of the room into the kitchen. The pot was empty, so she put the kettle on, hearing the rumble of voices behind her, and then, clearly, over the others, Lucas's voice.

"I'll just take this suitcase on to my room first."

A shiver went down her spine as she listened to his dearly loved voice. Oh, what was wrong with her that she had to fall in love with a man who couldn't make her happy — whom she couldn't make happy! Why couldn't she have loved Brent Allan? He was firmly and contentedly established in the restaurant business with his father. He loved Fairhill as much as she did.

Grace and Angus came into the kitchen, Grace giving her another searching look.

Kristen was ready for it this time. She smiled back casually and was relieved to see Grace's face relax. "I put the kettle on."

"Good. I swear, I can't think straight tonight, Kristen. I feel so distracted I'm about to jump out of my skin. I guess coffee is the last thing I need. Lucas looks good, doesn't he?"

Kristen nodded. "Yes, he does," she answered calmly. "And it's no wonder you're distracted, Aunt Grace, with the wedding tomorrow."

"I know — and I just know there's a million things I've forgotten to do."

"Come over here and sit down and relax," Angus said tenderly. "The only thing that matters, Gracie, is your standing up there tomorrow and promising you'll be my wife. Think you can manage that?"

A knife turned in Kristen's chest as she watched the look of deep love and devotion that passed between her aunt and Angus. Grace reached over and put her hand on top of Angus's. He swiftly turned it over and enclosed it. "You're right, Angus," she said softly, her eyes shining. "That's really all that matters, and I can do that, I promise you."

A sound from the hall made Kristen lift her head. Lucas stood in the doorway, a stricken look on his face. It must match the one on her own, she thought, pain filling her as she turned away to grab the whistling kettle and make the coffee.

"Dearly beloved, we are gathered here —"

Kristen's eyes filled with tears as she listened to the beautiful words of the wedding service. Lucas stood beside her, so close that the sleeve of his suit brushed the sleeve of her rose-pink dress.

Somehow she'd gotten through the rest of the

previous evening, pleading a headache and fleeing to bed as soon as possible. She'd even managed to survive this morning, sharing breakfast with Lucas and Angus and Grace.

Angus and Grace were so wrapped up in each other they seemed to see the world around them in a rosy haze. Kristen had taken care not to look directly at Lucas, not to meet those deep blue eyes that could see to the depths of her, read the love she harbored for him. She sensed that Lucas was waiting for a chance to get her alone, and she saw to it that never happened.

There had been one bad moment just before the music started from the small piano in the sitting room, when Kristen had been helping Grace dress. Her aunt had looked radiantly happy and ten years younger in her soft blue-violet dress, her hair in a loose, flattering arrangement.

Her hazel eyes had lost their dreamy, starry look and had sharpened as they focused on Kristen. "Honey, I've been so flustered with all this wedding stuff that I haven't even asked if you and Lucas have been able to talk. But I don't guess you have, there hasn't been time."

Kristen smiled at her aunt, avoiding her eyes. "No, we haven't had time," she said evasively, turning to adjust a fold of her aunt's skirt.

"Well, there's going to be time after all this is over," Grace said. "I saw the way you two were looking at each other last night — nothing's changed there."

So it had been that obvious, had it, in spite of everything? Kristen swallowed a lump that suddenly came up in her throat. "Yes, there'll be plenty of time after the wedding," she said, her voice raspy.

Grace patted her hand. "Honey, don't be so worried. When two people really care about each other, there's usually some way to work things out."

Not when they both want totally different lifestyles, she answered her aunt silently. "Yes, you're right, and now I want you to stop thinking about anything except your wedding," she had told Grace firmly, somehow keeping her smile intact.

Now it was almost over. Soon Grace and Angus would get into the taxi, go to the airport at Fenton's Corners, and be off on their honeymoon. And then Lucas could pick up his suitcase and once again leave Fairhill — this time for good.

How she was going to endure the rest of her life without him, she didn't know. But she'd do it. She had her work and she had Fairhill, the place she wanted to live. She was in good health and had enough money to live on. Lots of people never had that much in a lifetime.

Chapter Ten

Lucas, his jaw set, watched Kristen hurry upstairs as soon as they'd seen his father and Grace off in the taxi. She'd made it plain since he'd arrived last night that she still felt as she had when he left, and she'd managed to avoid being alone with him. Well, that was about to change. She could stay upstairs for an hour, but when she came back down, he was going to be here waiting for her.

Because he'd seen something else in her eyes last night, and today too. She still loved him, he was sure of that. And he was going to talk to her all night, if necessary, to convince her they belonged together. He reached into his jacket pocket to touch the ring box again, to be sure it was still there.

Why on earth did he love such a hardheaded woman, he asked himself for the dozenth time since yesterday. For love her he did, and right now, watching her slim, erect figure walk up the stairs, he wanted to go after her, if necessary pick her up in his arms and carry her off to Pittsburgh, build her that house she'd love. She wouldn't have to struggle with this shop any longer, worry about making a go of it.

The front door opened, and he turned to see

who it was. A woman came in and closed it behind her, smiling at him. "I didn't mean to disturb you, Lucas," she said apologetically, "but I forgot to pick up my check. Is Kristen around?"

He recognized her as Thelma Morgan, the woman who had been working in the shop and was going to take Grace's place. "She's upstairs, Thelma," he said, relaxing his jaw and returning her smile. "I'm sure she'll be down in a minute."

"I'll just wait then, if you don't mind." She walked on into the craft room and sat down in one of the chairs.

"No, of course I don't mind," Lucas answered.

"Wasn't that a lovely wedding?" Thelma asked after a few moments of silence.

Some inflection in her voice made Lucas realize that she — and probably the entire town — had expected him and Kristen to marry and was wondering what had happened. "Yes, it was," he agreed. "Angus and Grace make a great couple. Grace seems like my own aunt." He glanced up the stairs again.

"Grace is a wonderful woman, and so is Kristen," Thelma said. "They've helped us out so much by letting me bring my things in to sell here, and now giving me this part-time job in the shop. The farm isn't doing too well right now. Jim has had to get a job too," she added.

Lucas glanced at her, surprise going through him. He'd never thought of the shop in those terms, that Kristen and Grace were helping other people. He'd thought of it solely from their point of view, as a way for them to try to make a living — and not a very secure one, at that.

"Yes, this shop has helped out a lot around here," Thelma continued, unbuttoning her heavy winter coat. "A lot of the farm women who can't go out to work for some reason bring their craft items and preserved goods in here to sell. A lot of us are sure glad Kristen loves this old town so much she didn't decide to close the shop and go back to Baltimore when Grace got married."

Lucas's attention was riveted on Thelma now. Of course he'd known Kristen loved the town — heaven knew she'd told him often enough. He'd known she loved the life she lived here. But just the same, he'd come back here planning to convince her to marry him and move to Pittsburgh. He hadn't given a thought to what he might be doing to her if he *could* convince her.

Maybe she'd agree because he knew she still cared for him, in spite of her anger. He could tell that from those glances she hadn't been able to hide completely. But how long would their love last if he took her away from everything here that she loved? Another jolt of surprise went through him as he admitted something else: Kristen's work here was every bit as important and satisfying to her as his was to him. He couldn't imagine giving up Murray, Incorporated, and settling down here in Fairhill. He couldn't imagine Kristen asking him to.

But he'd thought nothing of asking that of her.

156

That was pretty selfish of him, he saw now. Maybe she'd be better off if he got out of her life for good. She'd eventually marry Brent Allan, or someone like him, who had his roots firmly here in Fairhill.

Now that he was thinking clearly about all this, those must be the reasons Kristen was treating him so coolly. She wasn't still angry — he knew she wasn't one to hold a grudge. She was just more sensible than he. That thought gave him another jolt. He had always prided himself on his levelheadedness, his good common sense.

He sharply remembered that night he'd first taken her out, when he'd lain awake for hours telling himself that he'd never let his heart rule his head. Well, he'd sure forgotten that, hadn't he? He hadn't had a clear, reasonable thought about the two of them since their quarrel.

Until now. Ironically it was now Kristen who was being sensible, who knew it could never work between them, given the totally different life-styles they both wanted — had to have, to be happy.

That was why she'd headed upstairs as soon as Grace and Angus left, and why she hadn't come back down. She didn't want to get into a long, futile discussion. She'd made it as plain as she could that she didn't want to have anything else to do with him.

It was a good thing he'd realized the truth now. He could get out of here without an awkward, embarrassing scene where she would have to come out and tell him again, as she had the night she'd given him back his ring almost as soon as he'd put it on her finger, that she was finished with him. He glanced up the stairs again. Kristen was still in her room.

"If you'll excuse me, Thelma," he said, "I have to be leaving. Will you tell Kristen I had to go?"

Thelma stared at him in surprise. "Why, yes, of course, Lucas," she said. "But don't you want to tell her yourself?"

Lucas shook his head. "No, I can't wait." He didn't dare wait. If he did, he'd probably try, in spite of everything, to convince Kristen they could make it work. He turned and hurried to his room, quickly repacking his overnight case. In five minutes he was out the door and pulling away from the curb.

Kristen, coming back downstairs, heard the sound of the motor starting, and she stopped, a shaft of pain going through her. Lucas was leaving, then, without even saying good-bye. Of course that was best, she told herself numbly, slowly resuming her walk down the stairs. That last silly bit of hope she'd had that maybe they could work something out was just that — silly.

Lucas had done the best thing. Cut it off clean and final. She entered the craft room and saw Thelma. "Oh, I didn't know you were here." She managed some kind of smile.

The other woman stood up, smiling anxiously. "Yes, I forgot my check, and since tomorrow is Christmas and we won't have the shop open for a few days —"

"Of course. I put it in the drawer here." Kristen walked to the counter and opened one of the shallow drawers.

"Lucas asked me to tell you he had to leave," Thelma said, walking to stand by the counter. "He seemed in an awful rush."

Kristen drew in her breath sharply, feeling the pain go through her again. "Thank you, Thelma. I guess something came up suddenly." She handed Thelma her check.

"I guess so." Thelma lingered, plainly wanting to talk, but Kristen couldn't stand any more of this.

"Well, you have a good Christmas, Thelma, and I'll see you in a few days."

"Merry Christmas to you too, Kristen," Thelma said warmly. "Are you going to stay here all by yourself?"

Kristen nodded firmly. "Yes, I am. I'll be visiting with friends, though, so don't worry about me."

"Well, that's good. I'll be running along now."

Kristen watched her go, the shop bell jangling behind her in a final kind of way. She walked to the front window and pulled the curtains aside. A few snowflakes came lazily down, melting almost as soon as they touched the ground. The weather forecast called for snow tonight, she remembered.

Snow on Christmas Eve. She should be happy and contented, she told herself. Here she was snug in this house she loved, in this town she loved — all set to live the life she wanted to live. And she was totally, completely miserable.

Her thoughts went to Grace and Angus, by now on the plane to New York, where they'd stay for a few days before leaving for Europe. Their happiness had been almost incandescent. Grace hadn't given a second thought to leaving this house, this town she'd lived in all her life. All her energies were focused on Angus and the life they'd have together. She hadn't even given a backward glance, but had gone confidently ahead into the future.

Kristen thought of Lucas, driving back to Pittsburgh, as alone as she was. She'd been almost certain that he planned to insist they talk this thing out. That was why she'd lingered so long upstairs, trying to get her courage high enough to confront him and tell him he might as well leave. They'd already made the decision that night they quarreled, and nothing had changed. They still wanted totally different kinds of lives.

The image of Lucas, alone in his car as she was alone here in this house, filled her mind until nothing else mattered. She sucked in a deep breath as a shock of realization went through her. Nothing else *did* matter! Grace and Angus

160

had proved that, hadn't they? If you thought about it logically, they were a most unlikely couple, but they would make it work — she knew they would. Just as she and Lucas could somehow make their own relationship work if they both really tried.

She hadn't been bravely facing up to what had to be, she saw now — just the opposite, in fact. She'd been a coward. She, Kristen Edwards, who prided herself for her outspoken honesty and courage, had been afraid to try. She'd come home from Baltimore, fed up with the dog-eat-dog life of real estate, and settled in contentedly here, away from all the strife. Then Lucas had come, shaking up her safe little world. And she'd closed her eyes to reality, tried to fit him into her life here. But it hadn't worked, of course, because Lucas needed that larger world.

And she needed Lucas. "So why are you standing around here?" she said aloud, wheeling away from the window. She grabbed her purse and flung on her running sweatshirt. Morris wandered in, giving her an inquiring look and meow.

"I'll be right back," she told him, crossing her fingers. "With company, I hope." She opened the door and then closed it again, glancing back toward Lucas's room. She'd almost forgotten one very important thing.

She hurried to Lucas's room and went inside. Five minutes later, carrying a package wrapped in cheerful Christmas paper, she let herself out

161

the front door again. She hurried out to the station wagon, keeping her fingers crossed that it would start. It could be balky in cold weather. To her relief, it did start, and she maneuvered it carefully onto the street.

The snow was coming down harder, she saw, but never mind. Lucas had only about a half hour's head start; he couldn't have gotten too far. Once on the interstate she drove as fast as she safely could, overtaking and passing other, more cautious drivers.

Forty-five minutes later, she had to admit she was licked. Snow was falling so thick and fast that even with the windshield wipers going full speed, she could barely see the road. Even if she could overtake Lucas, which now seemed like a crazy idea, she probably couldn't see his car well enough to recognize it.

Tears blinding her eyes, she took the next exit and, carefully and slowly now, headed back to Fairhill. It just wasn't meant to be, she tried to comfort herself. So she'd just go home, make a roaring fire and sit beside it, and open the bottle of wine she'd bought for Christmas dinner.

By the time she finally reached her own street, the weather could only be called a blizzard. With a sigh of relief, she parked in the driveway and got out, taking her gift-wrapped package with her. She put her key in the lock and turned it, then frowned as she saw the door hadn't been locked. Had she forgotten it in her haste?

Probably, she decided, shrugging, as she went

inside the warm house. Not that it mattered. She couldn't remember when there had been a burglary or robbery here. She laid her package on the hall table, then sniffed. Wood smoke. She knew she hadn't left a fire going in the kitchen.

A small chill went up her spine as she hesitated, and then Lucas appeared in the kitchen doorway. Her heart stopped beating for a moment. They stared at each other, then she blurted out, "Lucas, what are you doing here? You're supposed to be halfway to Pittsburgh by now." To her chagrin, her voice didn't sound welcoming or even warm, just upset and surprised.

He stared at her for a long moment, then a wry smile curved his mouth upward. "In case you hadn't noticed, it's snowing outside. I realized I couldn't make it any farther without risking getting stranded along the highway, so I thought I'd better come back while I still could."

"Oh. Yes, of course." Kristen nodded woodenly. For a wild moment there, she'd thought he was going to say he'd come back because he couldn't leave her, because he couldn't stand life without her. *Well, go on,* her mind prodded her. *That's what you were racing madly after him to tell him, wasn't it? So go ahead, do it!*

Somehow, though, she couldn't. It had seemed so easy when she'd thought of it, just find Lucas and tell him how much she cared for him and how they could work something out. But suppose she was wrong? Suppose she'd misread all the signals? Suppose he didn't love her anymore? After all, he hadn't tried to talk to her, had he? He'd just up and left. And just because she thought she knew the reason why, didn't mean she did. Her batting average for being wrong was hitting a thousand lately.

Instead she asked, "Where's your car? I didn't see it out front."

"I left it down at the Texaco station. It was giving me a little trouble on the way back. You're wet — don't you want to take off that shirt?" He reached over and unzipped the sweatshirt, and helped her ease it off. "Where have you been?"

The touch of his hands on her arms made her shiver. She hoped he hadn't noticed. "Oh, just out visiting friends. Christmas Eve, you know." She evaded his eyes so that he couldn't read in them that she wasn't telling the truth.

There was a silence, then Lucas said, "Come on, I've got a good fire going in the fireplace. You need to get warm." His voice sounded more distant all the time.

She followed him to the kitchen, where a crackling fire gave out welcoming heat, and held her cold hands out to the blaze, while Lucas added another log. Morris, curled in Grace's rocking chair, opened one amber eye and then closed it again.

"It looks as if we may be in for a real blizzard," she finally said to ease the lengthening silence. "I could hardly get back home myself."

"Yes, I'm afraid so. You may be stuck with me for a while. At least until tomorrow." Lucas's voice was cool, and he gave her an intent look, as if he was waiting to hear what she would say to that remark.

Kristen shrugged awkwardly, feeling more ill at ease by the minute. He didn't have to act as if he couldn't wait to get away from Fairhill. She knew he wanted to. "It can't be helped, I guess."

Lucas's eyes seemed to get colder. "No, isn't that a shame?" His voice sounded even cooler now.

Kristen swallowed. She didn't know how to answer that. He was acting as if being here with her was the worst thing that could happen to him.

Another awkward silence fell. She pushed her hair back and gave him a direct look. Well, he certainly didn't have to worry. Just as soon as the weather cleared up, he could be on his way! "Have you had anything to eat tonight?"

He shook his head. "No, but I'm not hungry."

"*I* am," she said crisply. "I'm going to scramble some eggs. You're welcome to eat with me." She wasn't hungry either, she was too upset to be, but she knew she'd better eat something.

He didn't answer, and Kristen, her head high, walked over to the stove and got out one of the big iron skillets. She rummaged in the refrigerator for ham and eggs and butter. Out of the corner of her eye she could see Lucas standing by the fire, that stony look still on his ruggedly handsome face.

Now that she felt sure Lucas's love for her had died, why did this storm have to happen to keep them shut up here alone together? For maybe a couple of days? As if in answer to her unspoken thoughts, a hard gust of wind hit the house, spattering snow against the windowpanes.

"It's ready," she called in a few minutes, dishing up the fluffy eggs and savory slices of ham and putting them on the table. She poured coffee and sat down. In a moment Lucas came over, sitting down across from her.

Another hard blast of wind-driven snow hit the windows. Kristen shivered, and Lucas looked up. "Looks like this is going to be a big one."

His voice seemed to have thawed a little. What did that mean? Kristen nodded. "Yes. I wonder if Angus and Grace got off all right."

"Yes, I called the airport. Their plane took off before all this started."

"Good. I'd hate to think they'd have to spend the night in the airport."

"Me too. That wouldn't be a very nice way to start off your honeymoon."

Kristen drew in her breath sharply at his last words. It could just as well have been their honeymoon, too. If only. . . . She gave him a quick glance.

Lucas's eyes were intent on her, unwavering, as if he'd been having the exact same thoughts.

Kristen dropped her gaze to her plate and hurriedly finished eating. She pushed her chair back and picked up her plate. "Go ahead, take your time," she said, taking her plate to the sink. She quickly washed it and put it in the drainer to dry. "I'm tired. I think I'll go to bed."

Lucas glanced up from his coffee cup. "Good night, Kris. Merry Christmas." His deep voice softened on the last words.

Kristen swallowed a huge lump that suddenly formed in her throat. She had to get out of here. "Good night, Lucas," she answered, her voice trembling a little. "Merry Christmas to you too." She didn't look at him as she hurried out and up the stairs to her room.

Once she was in her nightclothes, she found she couldn't sleep. She heard sounds from downstairs for a while, as if Lucas were moving around. Then there was silence.

She thought of the Christmas tree that she and Grace had decorated for the craft room, and the gaily wrapped gifts underneath it that Angus and Grace had left for her. She'd always loved Christmas above all holidays since she was a child. This would be the first one she could ever remember that she wished was over and done with.

Lucas would have some gifts under the tree too, she knew. Grace had made sure of that, because she was hoping he'd stay on after they left. Well, he had, but not for the reasons she and her aunt had wanted him to. He was down there in his old room only because of the snowstorm. As soon as that stopped, he'd be on his way again, back to Pittsburgh.

This was the last chance she'd have to try to make things right between them. Of course they'd see each other again, with Grace and Angus married, but it wouldn't be like this. She should have told him the truth when she came back and found him here. Was it possible that he'd mistaken her surprise at seeing him for displeasure?

Another thought occurred to her, suddenly, making her sit bolt upright in bed. Could it be possible that she'd been right earlier, when she'd thought for a moment that Lucas, too, had decided to give their relationship another, final chance and had come back not because of the storm, but to talk to her?

Her breath caught in her throat at that thought, even as she denied it. She picked up a book, but the idea had lodged in her brain and wouldn't go away. It was a long shot, true, but it was the only one left. What did she have to lose? Finally she got up and put on her robe, and went quietly back downstairs.

A light still shone under Lucas's door, she saw to her relief. Maybe he was having trouble sleeping too. She walked down the hall and picked up the gift-wrapped package she'd left on the table by the front door, then went into the craft shop. She took a deep breath of the fragrant, pine-scented air and then, with a wry smile on her face, plugged in the tree lights. If she was going to do this, she might as well go all the way.

With all the other lights out, the room looked cozy and warm, cheerful and pretty with the Christmas decorations she and Grace had put up. Kristen knelt and placed her package on the edge of the pile of gifts.

She stayed there for a few moments, delaying what came next in her plan. This had been the easy part. Going over and knocking on Lucas's door and asking him to come in here was going to take considerably more nerve.

A small noise behind her made her glance up quickly. Lucas stood there holding a gift-wrapped package, his face mirroring the surprise that must have been present on hers.

Kristen scrambled to her feet. "Wh-what are you doing here?" she asked him, then could have kicked herself for using the same words she had earlier.

Lucas's lips turned up a little, showing just a hint of his dimple. "I could ask you the same thing."

Kristen nodded, staring at him. Finally she took a deep breath. All right, enough of being a coward about this. This time she'd tell him the truth about how she felt. She had nothing to lose, she reminded herself.

She gestured to the small package under the tree. "I came down to leave this for you. I was just getting ready to go knock on your door," she finished.

"That's a coincidence. I brought this for you —" He extended the package, and she took it automatically. "And then I'd planned to knock on your door too." He looked at her intently.

Kristen glanced at the small package in her hand, then reached down and picked up the one she'd placed under the tree a few moments ago. "Here, this is for you."

They stood there, looking at each other. Finally Lucas said, "As long as we're up, we might as well get comfortable. You can't open Christmas presents unless you're sitting on the floor by the tree." He sat down, one of the long-needled branches brushing his shoulder.

Kristen wet her dry lips and nodded. "You're right." She, too, sat down on the carpet. Now that Lucas was here, actually holding the package and ready to open it, she was overcome by doubts. What on earth had made her do that? Would he laugh at her? Fling the gift back in her face and tell her it was too late for that?

She placed the package Lucas had just handed her on the floor and reached for one of the other ones. At least she could delay this a little. "Here, this is for you too." With a small smile, she handed him a package Grace had wrapped.

Lucas took the package, then put it back under the tree. "Kristen, let's stop all this sparring; I want you to open the package I gave you."

Her eyes met his, then she dropped her gaze. "All right," she agreed, finding his gift again. Loosening the tape holding the paper together, she kept her eyes down. She couldn't stand to watch as Lucas opened the package she'd given him. What expression would be on his face when he saw it? Finally the wrapping was spread out before her, and she blinked in surprise. Somehow she must have mixed up the gifts and opened the one she'd wrapped for Lucas.

She glanced quickly at him. "Lucas, I think —"

He looked up at her, a stunned look on his face. "Kristen, what does this mean?"

She blinked, and saw that the package he'd opened contained exactly the same thing hers did — several sheets of paper. She looked back down at her package and gave it a closer scrutiny. Then she drew in her breath. The beautifully sketched Victorian house on the top sheet was the same as the one she'd given Lucas — except that the writing in the corner was different: *To Kristen with all my love. To be built wherever in Fairhill you want it.*

She felt tears pricking her eyelids. The house plans she'd given Lucas, the ones he'd left in his room, said almost the same thing — with one important difference. She'd told him to build it on the lot in the Pittsburgh suburbs. She gestured at the papers she held. "It means the same thing that this does, I guess. That I don't care where we live, as long as we're together."

They both moved at the same time, until they were sitting side by side. Lucas reached for her, and she raised her face for his kiss.

When it ended, he moved back and looked at

her tenderly. "Do you remember that old story, 'The Gift of the Magi'?" he asked her.

Kristen nodded, understanding lighting her eyes. "Yes. They each gave up their most prized possession to make the other happy. Their love was all that mattered."

Lucas smiled at her tenderly. "Yes, it was. But in our case, I don't think the price of love will be that high. I can work out of an office here half the year, if you think you can stand Pittsburgh the other half."

"Of course I can. Thelma would love to run the shop during those months."

"Do you think we'd be considered terribly eccentric if we built two houses just like this?"

Kristen smiled back, understanding dawning. "One here, and one in Pittsburgh?" She shook her head. "No, and who cares, anyway? I don't mind being considered a little odd."

"I don't either." He fumbled in his pocket and drew out a small box — a very familiar box. "I don't believe I've ever actually asked you to marry me. Kristen Edwards, I love you, and I want you to be my wife," he said formally, but his eyes were twinkling.

"Lucas Murray, I love you too, and I accept your proposal," Kristen answered in kind, but her eyes, too, were dancing. She held out her left hand.

Lucas took the ring out of the box and slid it onto her finger, then pulled her to him for another long kiss. "I didn't come back because of the blizzard. I could have found a motel along the road. I came back because I had to try one more time to talk to you."

She grinned at him. "And I didn't go out to visit friends this evening, either. I was coming after you, but I did get stopped by the snow."

He shook his head, grinning back. "When you came in that door tonight, you looked so hostile I was certain you wished I'd stayed away!"

"I was just surprised, but then you got so cool, I was sure you were telling the truth about the blizzard, and I didn't have the nerve to admit I'd been chasing after you."

"The chasing's ended." Lucas gently brushed her hair back from her forehead. "I'll never let you go again."

As the snow still fell silently outside and the colored lights from the tree shed their magical glow over the scene, they sat, arms around each other, wrapped in contentment.

"I'll never want to leave," Kristen said, her love shining in her eyes.

The employees of G.K. Hall hope you have enjoyed this Large Print book. All our Large Print titles are designed for easy reading, and all our books are made to last. Other G.K. Hall books are available at your library, through selected book-stores, or directly from us.

For information about titles, please call:

(800) 257-5157

To share your comments, please write:

Publisher
G.K. Hall & Co.
P.O. Box 159
Thorndike, ME 04986